Index page

Richard Pochinko : Clown thru Mask

- 1. Title Page
- 2. Thank you
- 3. Index
- 4. Introduction
- 6. History of the Origins - Meeting Richard
- 16. Twelve Essential Exercises
- 18. Walking and Running to the Wall
- 20. Entering the Room
- 22. Looking for a Feeling
- 24. Return to Childhood
- 26. Neutral
- 28. Color
- 30. Six Impulses
- 32. Waving Goodbye to Someone you love
- 34. Facing Yourself in Six Direction
- 36. Mask-Making & Painting
- 38. Mask-Making & Cluster
- 40. 7th Mask
- 42. Clown Turns
- 44-47 6 in one mask workshop - design Ian Wallace
- 48-61 Clown Photos (Many thanks to Douglas Wallace)
- 62-63 Ian Wallace
- 64 Jan Henderson
- 67-77 Della's Student Clown Diary by Della Burford
- 78-81 Pat Brennan - Reflections
- 82-83 Richard Pochinko
- 84-85 Jan Grygier
- 86-92 Clown Registry
- 93- 96 Naomi Tyrell, Jan Kudelka,
- 97- 98 Melissa Aston
- 99 Dream with Ian - Della

INTRODUCTION TO MASK/CLOWN POCHINKO TECHNIQUE
Quotes from Ian Wallace

"Creativity, innovation, and the need for inspiration is common to the human experience. This book is for people from all walks of life who have a desire to connect and play with their creativity. No previous experience or training is necessary."

"Based on the technique evolved by Canadian visionary Richard Pochinko, it is a form of creative exploration drawing on three traditions: American circus clown, European clowning and Amerindian trickster/mask."
'

"This is an internal mask process with emphasis on communication, gesture, body language and voice. It is a book of self-discovery, a way in to the creative source using your unique energies to create a clown/trickster."

"Participants will be guided through the following series of lessons which are 12 essential exercises including mask-making which will awaken and encourage the ability to trust your inner voice, increase awareness, and develop an honest response to internal impulses as well as external events."

"Together we evolved creative work which is not only for actors but everyone. It's designed to help people get in touch with their childhood, with their inner sense. It's process of bypassing the thought process of the head, which people most of their lives are coming from. Getting in touch childhood is probably the most important element. People lose this very quickly because children soon want to be like everyone else and "What they are, what makes them different they hide.
 It is those differences we go through the mask process to rediscover and celebrate through presentation, performance, and life."

Richard Pochinko: Clown thru Mask

Method Design © Richard Pochinko

"A Brief History and Evolution of the Work and Lessons"

With Lessons compiled by Ian Wallace
(Ian also got advice from Jan Henderson)

Intro & History by Ian Wallace

Production by Della Burford, Dale Bertrand and Ian Wallace for Azatlan

Book Design: Ian Wallace
Della Burford & Dale Bertrand

Historical photos by Douglas Wallace

Jaquie Howardson - copy editing

Azatlan Publishing
I.S.B.N. 978-1-927825-06-8

Della's Student Clown Diary
© Della Burford 2018
Pat's Reflections ©Pat Brennan 2018

Thanks to: In memory R.I.P Dec 13th 2017 Ian Wallace ..in gratitude for his wise words, gentle way and inspiration. This book was his idea to share the story of the beginning of the Pochinko Clown thru Mask technique . He was with Richard when the technique was created from visions and dreams and was told at the time it was to be a book. We are happy to help in the manifestation for him.
Della & Dale

"Some of the participants do not possess any of the theatrical backgrounds, but it doesn't matter. In fact, Mr. Wallace wants to see people from a variety of background in a workshop. "It always helps to have mixed variety, of women and men, old and young, of some people trained in the theatre."

"The mask making begins with the learning to bypass the mind and listen to the body through color work. It is the rhythm of the color.. the color within them that is actually expressing itself. They're being a channel for these particular energies, to the extent that they can. We do a lot of preparatory work of not listening to the head but to something deeper inside In a full clown workshop they go thru the elements, as well as below the center of the earth and up to the highest star imaginable. If you face north one axis runs through the body to the south, another runs east and west and the third from the earth to sky. Where these axis meet is your place in the universe, that's your sphere."
"Each axis is a key to open yourself up and from the rhythm and the sound of each direction."

"Whenever we work with the clay we internalize the statement above and work it with our fingers with our eyes closed. The clay draws that out of us in the form of the mask. When we keep our eyes closed we shut off all inner perceptions and allow the mask to be formed by feelings. Somewhere along the way, they face whatever is tucked away. In doing this we find what is unique.. that is what the clown is the most fully expanded form of expression and being."

"If you look back over the history of societies all over the world, particularly native culture, you always find a figure. In the native society it was called the Trickster or the Contrary and to some extent the medicine man. The job of the Trickster and Contrary was to toss everything up in the air, to make people laugh.. to not get too serious about life, death or themselves."

On Meeting Richard Pochinko
by Ian Wallace

Expo 67 - Montreal July 1967, rue St. Urbain

I was introduced to Richard Pochinko by Ellen Gautschi, writer director at George Williams University, who I met shortly after arrival in Montreal. Ellen said, "You must mrrt my friend Richard". She took me to his dark St Urbain basement apt. When we met the room lit up. When we met the space between and around us was glowing, golden, a halo of tangible light particles, it was uncanny, something I had never before experienced. All- encompassing peace and heightened awareness of belonging and accepting. My thought was, "This is a remarkable meeting".

He was all excited about this new vinyl raincoat from work at the Expo thearte where he was one of the 12 stage managers. The sparkle in your eyes, I can see it now and smile- I remember you telling me about driving Maurice Chevalier out to the stage in a little golf cart - he said, "you know, smiley, I've been doing this for close to sixty years and I still get afraid every time". I have the picture of you and Boris with Chevalier - I found it while cleaning out your desk. That photo was taken the same year that we met.

Boris. Chevalier, Pochinko Expo 67, Montreal

The beginnings of the
Richard Pochinko Clown thru Mask

We were becoming friends. Richard had fallen asleep, I was still awake when he started stroking his forehead and began speaking to me. He said that we were co-pilots and we were on a rescue mission, that we were flying a ship over a landscape looking for people. I answered him in co-pilot language, he gave me instructions and I carried them out steering the ship in various directions on the search. That first time we never found anyone. This turned out to be a recurring event, happening 4 or 5 times in 2 months. He talked about other people in the ship that we had already rescued, saying "some of them we know already and others we have yet to meet. The most vividly emotional and meaningful flight was when we were flying over a dark landscape with hills and valleys, he said "steer over to the left over that hill". I said "aye-aye sir" and made the movement. As we flew over the crest of the hill he saw some people off in the distance and got very excited, urging me to get closer. As we got closer his excitement heightened "Oh. Look. Look, They're waving at us!" he was so happy, but as we got closer he suddenly said "Oh God!, Oh my God!" he went from being extremely happy and excited to unbelievable shock and horror as we saw the people. In a trembling voice, almost in tears he said "they're not waving at us, they are all encased in glass tubes and they're banging on the glass trying to break out" then in a flash he said "Oh my God! That's our mission, that's why we are here – to set them free, to help them break out of the glass tubes." My dream life has been very active since I was a child but I never had a conversation with a sleeping person before. Richard and I were both fans of Edgar Cayce the "sleeping prophet" so it was an experience that I was ready to respond to and receive. At the time I did not realize the significance of these dreams and how they were a stunning metaphor for the work that we would eventually create, which has come to be known as Richard Pochinko Clown Through Mask.

Inspiration in Paris

On a typical day Richard would leave for the Le Coq studio at about 8 a.m and I would proceed to work on my set and costume designs for the 3 shows we were planning to do in Whitby with Ellen Gautschi when she returned to Canada. At the same time I was making batik paintings, having ventured all over the city trying to find beeswax and cold water dyes. When Richard arrived home from school I would cook the noodles on our singel burner and prepare the meal. Richard would usually lie down for a nap.
One day not long after we had moved in he lay down for his nap, I had the lamp burning on the table and I was finishing up some of my notes. I looked and noticed him with his eyes closed stroking his forehead with his right hand. This was not unusual for I had seen him do this before when he was having the space-ship dreams in Halifax and Toronto. However this time he suddenly sat up in the bed, opened his eyes and looked at me with almost a stunned look, like he didn't know where he was. He looked around the room and looked back at me and smiled. It was as if he was listening to someone. then he laughed. I thought it was like he was awake in a dream, then he started to speak to me in a child-like voice "My name is I, me, Richard, he, and if you tell Richard that this is happening he won't believe you" and he laughed again. I must have been a little dumb-struck because he told me not to be frightened , that he had some things to tell me, then he said that the light was too bright, he was shielding his head and eyes and asked me to turn off the lights and just have the oil lamp burning at a certain level. As I got up to fix the lights he cautioned "don't move so fast - you're shifting the energy too much." So I moved very slowly and carefully across the room then back to adjust the oil-lamp and sit at the table again. All the while he was watching me with these wild eyes and the face of a six-year old. Once the light from the lamp was right he explained to me that this was being allowed to happen because of the depth and strength of our love for each other. He proceeded to tell me what he was seeing. He looked at me and talked about the colors he saw around me. As he looked at the Lautrec prints on the walls he told me how perfect it was that they were there.
That the colors would be very important to us in the future. I now realize that they were to be the lighting effects for my show Nion, with one side of my face in green and the other in yellow or pink, just like the faces in the paintings I put up in the room He would look at me and answer a question that was in my mind,
that I had not spoken. (cont'd)

He tried to explain to me where he was speaking from. He used his hands to delineate ordinary human consciousness about a foot high, and with l.s.d. your consciousness was opened to about 7 feet high, but where he was speaking from right now beyond that. At one point he started smacking his lips and asked me to get him some water because his mouth was dry so I carefully got up and went to the sink , got water and held it out to him. Just at that moment he snapped out of it and there was Richard looking at me kind of like he just woke up. "what are you doing?" he asked. "I'm bringing you the water you asked me for", I responded. He looked at me kind of wierdly and said "but I've been sleeping." I said "Richard, I have something to tell you", and I told him what had happened, about I, me, Richard, he, and the little boy. He said "no, I don't want to hear this, it frightens me, I don't believe you, don't tell me any more." I said "that's what you told me you would say." He said "I can't listen to this." I said "Okay", and that was that for the time being. For the next three weeks the same thing happened at the same time every evening. He would lie down, start stroking his fore-head then sit up and talk to me. I felt like i was having a conversation with God. He talked of love, and energy, consciousness, theatre of the future, healing, our mission. He spent a lot of time speaking about thought projection and the transmission of energy. One night he was trying to describe the waves of light and color that he was seeing around me. He took my paints and started painting little dots of color but very soon got frustrated because it wasn't right so he crumpled up his paper.

Immediately a wave of concern came over his body, I could see him listening very seriously. "I've just done something really wrong and they're telling me I have to lie down." He lay down and stroked his forehead. "They're opening up a big book and in it they're showing me the preciousness of creativity. It's the most valuable gift we have been given, and by destroying my creation I went against one of the fundamental laws of the universe." I could see the emotions ripple through his body. He was like a little boy being lovingly chastised by his mother. It was amazing to witness because up to that point it had just been he and I. Now I was aware of the huge presence of a third which he referred to as "they". Suddenly the event took on a whole new dimension as I realized how privileged I was to witness and be part of this unusual communication and interaction.

Going to Canada to start a School of Masks and Clowns.

He said that we were going back to Canada to start a school of mask and clown, that it would be ahead of its time and would close after a year, but would be reborn and flourish some years later. This would later be the Theatre Resource Centre. "We will create a new, unique approach to clown through mask for the North American continent based on Amerindian reverence for Mother Earth and all living creatures. this was our mission and the teachers we train will be like missionaries. This is the planting of a seed that will grow into a major movement."

He foretold that I would have great success as a "clown", that the work would be ahead of it's time and not be accepted by every one, but that we would break the ground for those to follow. That I would find myself in a milieu of artists like the characters in the Lautrec paintings. He called me the "keeper of the house" and said that in the future I was to share this story with anyone who asked about it. This was the seminal origin of what has come to be called "Richard Pochinko Mask/Clown Technique". Some refer to it as "Canadian Clowning."

When we returned to Toronto in the spring 1971, Richard was very excited about the studies in Paris and was keen to experiment with teaching neutral and character mask moving into personal clown. He worked on forming a neutral from clay, and had me explore different materials for creating the actual masks, some were made with layers of tissue paper and glue, others I used cheesecloth and glue. Eventually we had about 7 masks ready to wear and use in classes. With the help of Marigold Charlesworth, actress and director at the N.A.C., meetings were arranged between Jean Roberts, head of the N.A.C., Ottawa and with the head of the St. Lawrence Centre, Toronto. Richard and Marigold proposed the creation of a Mask based Clown show, for their High School touring companies, the Hexagon the and Theatre Hour Co., both of which toured and presented shows and workshops in High Schools all over the province.

Actors would be auditioned to participate in a mask/clown training workshop, for one month in Toronto. Then Richard and Marigold would form the 2 companies, each working with 6 actors to create their own show around the same script, an adaptation of the Iroquois Creation Legend, researched and written by Rosalind Mayann. We were very pleased when we found that the proposal had been accepted, and we all set to work in a big studio on Queen St. East in Toronto. Training in neutral mask was the foundation of the work. In neutral, the actor finds a place of readiness by internalizing the words, Necessity, Economy and Universal. It is like a meditation, a total awareness of your being in stillness, movement and expression, bringing your awareness into the moment.Only the essence, nothing extra, with a sense that you are a Universal being, radiating light in all directions. The actors were also trained to present a ½ hour workshop for Theatre Students at every high school between Sarnia and Red Lake, including Toronto. We traveled in a Greyhound bus to one school in the morning-unloaded everything and set up our stage in the gym, do the show and workshops then strike everything back into the bus and move to another school in the afternoon. Both companies met in Sudbury and it was amazing to witness each others' show, same script but with a totally different interpretation and presentation We did this again the following season with a Shakespeare inspired script called "So Runs the World Away".

In the meantime Richard went to Seattle to take a mask/clown workshop with Bari Rolfe. However when he phoned me he was very excited about an encounter he had with a spirit guide at the Anthropological Museum. His name was "Jah-Smit" and he had previously appeared at the foot of our bed in Toronto, which had scared Richard. However in Seattle the guide instructed him to recognize a "mask" in a tree, waiting to be released. Jah-Smit told him to go out to the end of the wharf and wait there until he was able to see himself on the horizon. This was a crucial step in the development of the Pochinko Clown/Mask work. The experience encapsulated our work around facing yourself in each of the six directions, and sculpting 6 masks in clay with eyes closed using each "direction" as the focus.

Ian & Richard in Paris

Ian with Wendy Gorling, far left, and friends from the Le Coq Mime School, Paris 1970, photo by Richard

Richard & Friends at Le Coq Mime School, Paris 1970

Richard, Ian in Central Park, N.Y., July 4, 1984 New York Clown Festival organized by John Towsen.

Jah Smit as visualized by Ian

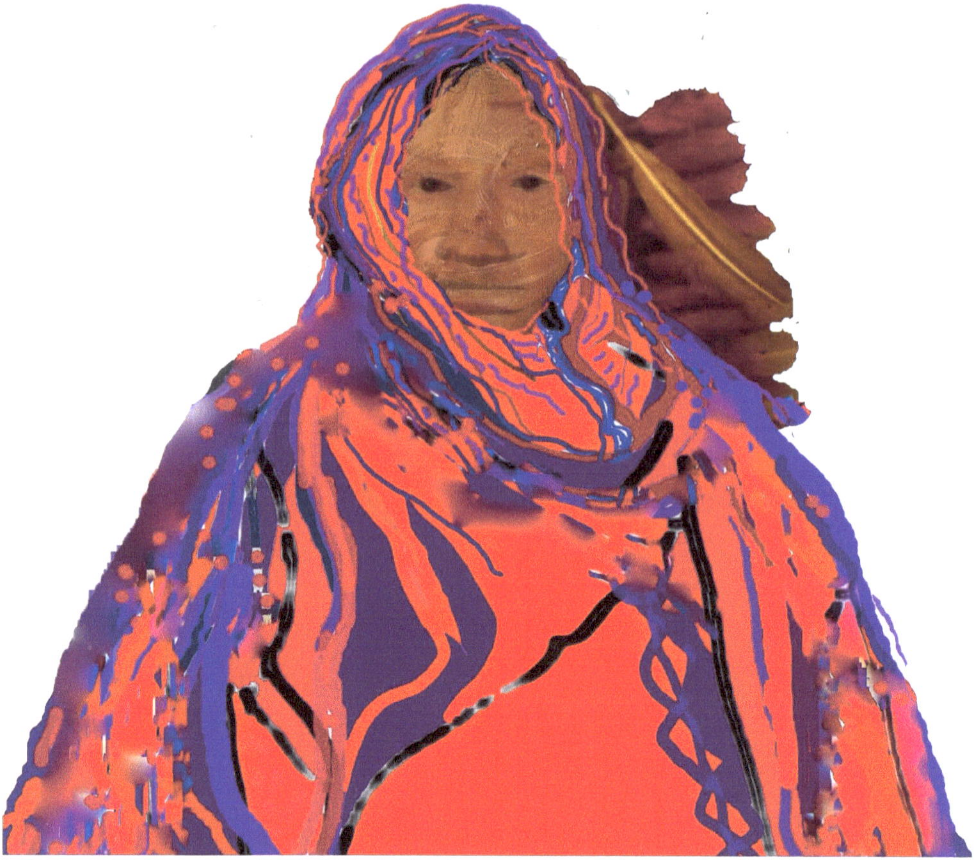

Jah Smit painted by Ian Wallace

Ian Wallace photo by Carlos Tello

The Beavers Promotional Photo

TWELVE ESSENTIAL ESSENTIAL EXERCISES

RICHARD POCHINKO

CLOWN THRU MASK

WRITTEN IN LOVING MEMORY
BY IAN WALLACE
with inspiration from
Richard Pochinko

This is dedicated
to the artists, clowns,
teacher/guides and friends
who have been inspired
to "know themselves"
by exploring this
Mask/Clown technique. There
is room for many in this exploration.
Best wishes to all! Ian wanted to
give special thanks to Jan Henderson

Thanks to:
Richard Pochinko who gave his inspired vision to help so many to be creative and Ian Wallace for his devotion to keep the legacy alive of the Pochinko Clown to Mask technique…. many send love to both!

WALKING AND RUNNING TO THE WALL

You and your guide are in an open large space with grass and trees or in a big studio with a wooden or cement floor.

You mark out a safe space and all the students take turns walking the length of the room.

You walk right to the far wall with your eyes closed. You see the space, it is clear.... each one goes in turn.

Quickly you see they are stopped by something, you laugh, this is walking through your fears.. .. don't let your fears stop you ,,, go directly to the wall, eyes closed. This is walking to the wall, then running to the wall with eyes closed. One at a time , each of the participants will be protector of the next participant running to the wall. After the walk or run to the wall, share your experience with others.

Jaguar Serpent Guardian by Ian Wallace's side.

ENTERING THE ROOM

One at a time each one exits the room you are in.
They enter the room individually by knocking
You do nothing, just enter and take the space
Share with each of the audience one at a time

If you have to take a little bit longer that is fine.
Don't do anything just feel the feeling of the contact.
Make contact with each one!
Share the feeling with each one briefly
You should stay long enough to let go
When you are completed stand back and
see them all as one.
Share this feeling
Celebrate this feeling!

Stand back and see them all as one. Group connect.

Wait for impulse to leave ! ! ! !
Leave - one last look before exit ! ! ! ! !

Group in Sicily with Ian Wallace

LOOKING FOR A FEELING OBSTACLE COURSE

The clown is not about being funny. It is important for you to navigate how you feel from one environment to another. Think of your life as an obstacle course or a series of events that may include trauma and a challenge but through this journey transformation is made. Best not to judge - this is your story. Map out your story.

Richard Pochinko

Return to Childhood

Exploring the Innocence of the Characterization

(This is the version that Richard shared with us from his time at L'École Jacques Lecoq.)

Think of a safe space where you played as a child, around 3 – 5-years-old. This should be a real place, whether indoors or outside. You could spend hours in this place, by yourself: with favourite toys, or maybe climbing trees... Remember and reflect on that place and time, when your job was to play.

You, as you are now, will go back to that place. You see the street, the house, or the space, and it is just as you remember it.
You, the adult, enters and finds everything as you left it. Notice the light, the scent, the sounds, the memories... Go to a room, attic, corner, the yard, etc. where you played.
Find a closet, drawer, or box: the container that holds all your toys and special things. As you take each one out, remember what it was like to play with it. Remember how much fun you had.

You will discover things you had forgotten. Play with the toys as the adult and when you find something that was really special, allow yourself to get lost in the play and slip back into being the child again. Discover the innocence and timelessness of the play. Allow yourself to remember songs, smells, qualities of light, patterns, colors and textures. Experience the joy of childplay, feel it and cherish it.

This exercise may be done individually or as a group. In a group setting, each student should choose a space in the studio where they can work uninterrupted. Once all participants have rediscovered their childplay, suggest that they venture out into the larger space to encounter others and begin to play with them.

Ian Wallace and Ellen Pearce at Theatre Resource Centre

Neutral Mask

The Neutral, or Universal, mask was originally developed as a learning tool for actors - to help develop emotional honesty, economy of movement, and to open an inner core that is balanced, centred and focused while they express powerful, authentic emotions on stage. Above all, a study of the Neutral Mask is research into the basics of movement and creation.

"There are three masks: the one we think we are, the one we really are, and the one we have in common." Neutral mask is "the one we really are", the one that allows us to take off all the other masks. "Neutral is holding the centre" - moving with grace, dignity, power, and direction. "To relax our attention into the present moment is extraordinarily simple, but, for most of us, it demands a lifetime of practice."
Jacques le coq

"Neutral mask allows those who wear it to get in touch with their core being, their most authentic, intuitive self. The mask encourages a sense of wholeness, of physical, emotional, and intellectual centeredness. In the mask, one lives in the moment, questioning nothing, yet empowered to make changes as needed. It integrates mind and body, clarifies impulse, and allows the wearer to experience the power and increased presence that come from absolute self-acceptance. Energy that formerly would be wasted on self-doubt and critical comments about a given situation is now used on problem solving. Neutral mask allows you to take off all the other masks."
Jan Henderson

A study of the neutral mask is a study of what binds us, what separates us, and how the two flow through the world outside of us. Above all, a study of the Neutral Mask is research into the basics of movement and creation. "We shall never cease from exploration And the end of all our exploring will be to arrive where we started and to know the place for the first time."
T. S. Eliot

When wearing the neutral mask, we attempt to enter a state of openness, a forward moving, physically engaged curiosity with the world around us. The mask is a tool through which we learn the elements of movement intentionality and technique. We experience a sense of wholeness and well-being. We may find ourselves doing unexpected things – being impelled to obey the choices imposed by the mask and finally being taken over by it.

"The concept of neutral or zero is needed to measure time, space, rhythm, force, and also personality for characterization is measured by it's departure from neutral. It frees the actor to discover what only exists in himself, that by cocking a sensitive ear he could hear in himself movements he could never have detected any other way ..
Peter Brook

Raecheli & Dawn in Sicily

Workshop in Sicily with Ian Wallace

COLOR (SPECTRUM, VISUALIZATON) AND MOVEMENT

*Expressing personal movement,
sound and emotions
triggered by the internal resonance
of different color vibrations.*

You should lie down comfortably with your eyes closed , breathe easily, and as you breathe in image of your world, let your whole body be filled with the clear white light - feel that light energy in every particle of your being.

When you are relaxed and comfortable with your eyes closed, imagine a glowing red ball at your forehead, Let it in and flow with your own body, the color RED, right to the tips of your toes and let your body go with the movement, Let there be a sound rhythm for the energy RED Let it take your whole body into standing and moving through the room , growing larger and explore the movement and rythm to your paper and paints and pastels.Express the feeling of RED and how it moves and moves you. Release and come back to neutral. Share your experiences. Eventually you should do each color of the rainbow. Finally after doing the colors you will do neutral with the four elements, Earth, Air, Fire and Water.

*Group walk .. breathing color into yourself
Jan Henderson, Allan Muse, Jexxica, Ellen
Pearce, Jan Millar*

SIX IMPULSES

"The six impulses are :

1. Be aware of what you are doing

2. Your body is aware your mind does not register

3. You become aware of change

4. Recognition of what is coming

5. It is coming toward you.

6. Attach or embrace.

Breath out of the hands and eyes.

Sara Tilley in front - workshop in Sicily with Ian Wallace

Waving Goodby to Someone you love

Exploring the experience of the character

AS YOURSELF - Make it a real person
Someone you love very much is leaving on a ship. They are going somewhere far away and you may never see them again. You have both discussed this and for whatever reason, you both agree that it has to be, and you know that this is for the best.

Improvisation Action
You are in your room, it is the night before and you are alone. You know that when you wake up in the morning you will be going down to the docks to say goodbye to your loved one. Experience the room - make everything as real as possible - be there with your thoughts and feelings. Undress and go to sleep. When the alarm rings it is morning and you prepare yourself, get dressed and step out through the door on your way to see your friend.
At this point the action stops, you close your eyes and visualize the following sequence.

Visualization - *In your minds eye, you see yourself making your way to the dock. You meet your friend, get them on the ship and say your good-byes. You see the boat start to leave and you see yourself start to walk back to your room. At this point the action begins again. Action - You are walking back from the dock through the city to your room, having waved goodbye to your friend. Allow your thoughts and feelings to be there. At some point in this journey you get an impulse to go back and wave to your friend one last time--if you don't follow the first impulse, there will be another. When you decide to go back there is an urgency because the ship may be out of sight so you run back to see your friend.*

When you get to the head of the dock you look out and see the ship. Look along the length of the ship until you see your loved one. You call out and you wave goodbye one last time, then when you are ready, you turn and walk away from the dock.
This is called EXPERIENCE

Linda Stephen - waving goodby to someone you love

Facing yourself in 6 Directions

1. Below, Below. (Feminine)

*See yourself as one with Mother Earth, creator of life,
provider of nourishment and sustenance. Send a wave
of light from your centre down through the layers of earth,
sand, rocks, insects, right to the very centre of the living
earth. See an image of yourself at the centre and imagine
growing into and filling the earth with your body, the
ground and trees are your skin, the water is blood, rocks your bones,
the wind is your breath, the fire is your heart, lose yourself
in the living Earth and let your body and voice move as
Mother Earth, receive her rhythms and
slowly start to express it in sound and movement, your
"song and dance" for below, below, the earth. once you feel connected
and open to the earth, relax back to neutral,
give thanks for what you received.*

2. East (New Beginnings)

*See yourself as a seed that has been planted in the rich, fertile
earth, feel the warmth and light of the sun and allow yourself to sprout.
As you emerge from the earth facing to the East see a beautiful
beach, the sunlight of a new day appearing on the
horizon, hear the song of birds heralding and celebrating
a new beginning. Send an image of yourself to the sun,
filling the space with your energy think of a "new beginning"
in your life and celebrate it here with a sound and gesture that
becomes your song and dance for the East. Receive the
opening to the East, relax back to neutral, give thanks for what
you received.*

*3. South (Energy) like a sunflower, turn and follow the rise
of the sun to it's highest point at noon, in the south. Feel
the heat and light energy of the sun in the south, see yourself
in the sun and, open and express the rhythm of the South,
back to neutral and give thanks for the gift of the South.*

4. West (Gentle Endings)
Continue to follow the sun to the West where the sun sets. see yourself on the horizon at the setting sun.
Gentle endings, what has come to completion in your life send it off to the west. Let your body make a gesture and a sound for this - let it evolve into a song and dance for the west. Let it go and give thanks for what you have received.

5. North (Mystery, Unknown) Continue turning 90 degrees to the right, you are facing North, in darkness for most of the year, mystery, the unknown. Project your image to the North, how do you approach the unknown in your life? Make a gesture, receive and express the rhythm, the sound, in a song and dance for the North, the gift of the North, for today. Again after you have received the opening from the North and expressed it in sound and movement, give thanks for what you have received.

6. Above, Above (Masculine) continuing the spiral, send a quantum wave of light up, through your body, out your head to the furthest star you can imagine, see yourself at that place, make a gesture and sound and reflect back the feeling of being above, above, let it fill you, making a song and dance for Above, Above, knowing that you have opened, return to neutral and give thanks for what you received.

Phyllis from the documentary Phyllis's Miracle

MaskMaking and Painting

Sculpting your own mask on clay with the eyes closed provides an opportunity to listen inside, and is a key to uncovering your creative source. The mask is then built using papier mache and paint, becoming a tool for self-discovery through a series of improvisations with emphasis on gesture,

You experince communication with body language and voice, bypassing the thought process.

Your mask leads you into the creation of a personal clown/trickster.

Mark Russell at the National Arts Centre

You should make an individual mask for each direction. Start with a neutral head-size lump of clay available. Mark on the clay where your eyes and nose would be. With the eyes closed internalize the sound/rhythm for that direction as above. Bring that movement through your fingers into every part of the clay, take no more than 5 minutes for this. Then come back to neutral. Re-internalize the rhythm, bring your fingers to the clay and change any parts of the mask which do not match the rythm. Come back to neutral.

This is called a checking process. Always with eyes closed. Continue this until no more changes are made -then you may open your eyes.

You will use this method to form 6 masks.

After the masks are made in clay you put paper maiche or soft tissue paper on for the mask to wear.

Masks from Jan Henderson workshop recently in Alberta.

Mask Wearing & Cluster

1. group attunement sanctify the space 2. power spot and small circle 3. charging your small circle 4. facing yourself in 6 directions 5. projection of polarities 6. return to childhood 7. waving goodbye to someone you love 8. mask exploration

Group attunement . Standing together in a circle in the centre of the room looking at each other, the community, reflecting Opening to the directions I like to start with grounding to the earth. See yourself standing on the Mother Earth, creator of life, provider of nourishment and sustenance. Send a quantum wave of light from your centre down through the layers of earth, sand, rocks, insects, worms right through to the very centre of the planet. Project an image of yourself right at the centre and reflect back to you standing, the feeling of this opening to the earth, allow your body to move and create sound for the feeling of being in the centre of the earth, receive the rhythm and express it in sound and movement, once you feel connected and open to the earth, give thanks for what you received and take that opening with you as you send a quantum wave of light up, through your body, out your head to the furthest star you can imagine. Project your image, see yourself at that place and reflect back the feeling of being above, above. Receive the gift as a rhythm of movement and sound in your body, let it fill you, know that you have opened and again give thanks for what you received. You are facing North. Project your image to the North, see yourself standing on the Earth, again, receive and express the rhythm, the gift of the North ,for today. The north historically has been the direction of Mystery, the Unknown, what do you see in your North mask? Again after you have received the opening from the North and expressed it in sound and movement, give thanks and turn 90 degrees to the right to address the East. The East, where the sun rises, see yourself facing the horizon at Sunrise, new beginnings, eagle, ...what do you see in your East mask?

Mask Wearing+ Cluster

Project your image through the space, reflect it back and receive and express the rhythm through sound and movement, give thanks for the opening and turn 90 degrees to the right to face South. South, heat , energy, red, coyote, rattlesnake...what do you see and feel from the south. If you have your mask.. what do you feel in it? Project, reflect, receive and express the rhythm of the mask of the South, know that you have opened and give thanks. Turn 90 degrees to the right and face to the West where the sun sets. see yourself on the horizon at the setting sun. Gentle endings, what gentle endings are happening in your life. Raven, whale, dolphin.. what do you see. What is in your west mask?. Project, reflect, receive and express this opening to the west in sound and movement, give thanks for this opening. Standing in the centre of your charged space, be aware of the three lines of energy going through your body. What do you see in your below.below and above/above masks? From below to above , from north to south, and from east to west. Where these three intersect that is your unique position in the universe, see yourself as a radiating point of light, going in and out, radiant and magnetic, this is your number 7 direction, (clown) For a moment go back to the direction that felt most unfamiliar to you. Spend a few minutes there and dialogue with that feeling and find out more about it, Then, after a couple of minutes go to the direction and mask that felt the most like home to you. Fill yourself with that strength and find out more about what is there for you. After this make a mind map with clusters coming from it about yourself. Get together with others and share in groups or clusters.

7TH MASK – CLOWN NOSE INTRODUCTION

Trickster/Clown (Innocence/Experience) Be aware of the three lines of energy through your body. Where these three intersect is your unique position in the universe.
Turn to the direction that felt most unfamiliar to you, spend a few minutes there and dialogue with that feeling. If there is an animal or color there let yourself open to what their message is. Then, after a couple of minutes go to the direction that felt the most like home to you, fill yourself with that strength, find out more about what is there for you, an animal or color to dialogue with. Go back to centre and be aware of opening your whole sphere in all these 6 directions, radiant, magnetic, in and out, radiant and magnetic. You should allow a song and dance to evolve letting any and all of these energies come out in sound and movement, spontaneous, unexpected, celebratory, within your safe circle. Add the clown nose.

You contain all these possibilities within your being! Take yourself to innocence and play! Individual directional energies may be used to help you play specific characters, or clowns. The mask is a tool to bring you inside to your creative potential. This is the beginning of your number 7 direction, (trickster/clown /zany/mischief maker.......)

CLOWNS TURNS

Go to the clothes box to find clothes and a hat

2. It a night before some you love is leaving .. wave goodby

3. From the original rythm wave goodby and then return to childhood

4. Find out what is fantastic and show it in a "clown turn"

Getting Ready to go to Circus - National Arts Centre

Finding the clown in the 6 in one
Teacher Ian Wallace

Group included Jan Grygier, Michael Diack, Morgan Nadeau, and M. Pyress Flame

All photos by Jan Grygier

The 6-in-1 Mask process for Pochinko's Clown Through Mask designed by Ian gives students a way to make all six directional masks/ energies with less time to think about it. This gives the students a way to get out of their head a lot easier. Each shape is created in one to two minutes within a guided sequence.

Each shape or totem will represent a direction, or impulse, of the student. They will explore the six directions of Below Below, East, South, West, North, and Above Above. Once all six of their totems are computed (over the span of about ten minutes) then they use a face shaped mould to piece together their mask.

You start with the totem that is calling out to be a nose and place that on the mould first. then you place the remaining 5 totems on the mask where they feel the most right. It is also important to create a mask map to aid you in remembering which direction is where on your completed mask. This will be important for the mask exploration later on. Once the Mask has been pieced together, you cover it with three layers of paper maché. Once the mask is dried, you de-clay it and paint the mask before exploration.

Ian Wallace's 6-in-1 Mask is beneficial for students who tend to be more in their head or students with limited time. Written by Morgan Nadeau

Ian Wallace with painting   *Ian Wallace & Jan Henderson*

Michael Diack & Morgan Nadeau working on the 6 in one mask workshop in Vanocuver with Ian Wallace

All photos in next three pages by Jan Grygier

The 6 in One Mask Process of Ian Wallace - by Michael Diack

    This exercise was one of many remarkable moments in two weekends of maskmaking and mask exploration with Ian Wallace, master clown teacher, in the summer of 2016. At the first weekend, Ian led us through an exploration of all directions that would be incorporated in the 6-in-1 mask we would create. East, West, North, South, Above-Above and Below-below. At the start of each direction, we assumed "neutral mask," then moved into finding the feelings, gestures, and images of each direction in turn.

    The first thing to come from each direction, for me, is a sound or song. It's vocalized through my throat, but originates, and is channeled from somewhere outside the known universe (perhaps deep inside me) - from the direction we're exploring. The song is tentative at first, but soon becomes clearer and more pronounced, as I move my body and walk & explore the landscape of the direction. Feeling comes next. Each direction has its own emotional territory, individual to each mask explorer. West for me is sad. East is energetic. South is sizzling, almost unbearably hot, like the surface of Mars, and the lack of oxygen makes me anxious as I try to breathe in the thin air. After feeling, and most importantly, Ian tells us, comes a gesture or movement. North makes me feel like I'm a stethoscope, snaking and moving. Above-above feels like being seasick on a boat in hurricane-strength seas. Below-below feels enormously happy and vibrant, like a dog greeting her master, arriving home from work. The gesture is extremely important, Ian tells us. It's the gesture, or movement - that we discovered in each direction - that we then place into the unformed clay of what will become our individual mask. Each of the six directions is "sculpted" into 6 different places on the 6-in-1 mask. Later, before each exploration of the completed mask, we'll spend a few moments feeling the direction on the mask with hands and fingers. Each ridge, ripple and line is alive with all the information and possibility contained in the direction we explored. Each place on the mask contains the essence of that direction.

    The following weekend, we paint the mask. Again, we start in "neutral mask," and Ian invokes us, one direction at a time, back into the six worlds. As he does this, the direction sound or song comes back. The gesture, miraculously, too is still there, very real. We are alive in that direction, once again. The images come clearly to me again - and this time, we add a strong sense of the colours of that direction. After a few minutes exploring that world, we go back to the mask. The direction place had been sculpted into the clay in the previous session. Now we paint the mask, each direction receiving the colours our exploration revealed. to me - Each person can be different. West is white. Below-below is red-green. South is red/orange. East is pink. Above-above is yellow. North is black.

    We'll do many more explorations with Ian, under his gentle and wise guidance, using the 6-in-1 mask. "Return to Childhood." "Waving goodbye." "The birth of our Baby Clown." But for me, the act of creation, the sculpting of the 6-in-1 mask, based on our own heretofore undiscovered worlds, is a spiritual and psychological exercise of profound personal import. It's no exagerration for me to say, that probably nothing in my life has given me the powerful and rich insights into my self and psyche, that the 6-in-1 mask has.

I'll be forever grateful to Ian, Richard Pochinko, Jan Hendersen and all other teachers and students, who continue in the Pochinko clown/mask tradition.

Painting the 6 in one Mask

Ian Wallace

Ian painting his mask

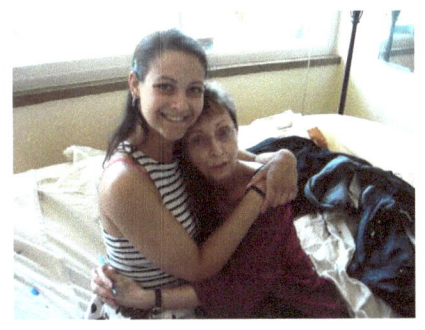 

Jan & Morgan

All photos by Jan Grygier

CLOWN PHOTOS

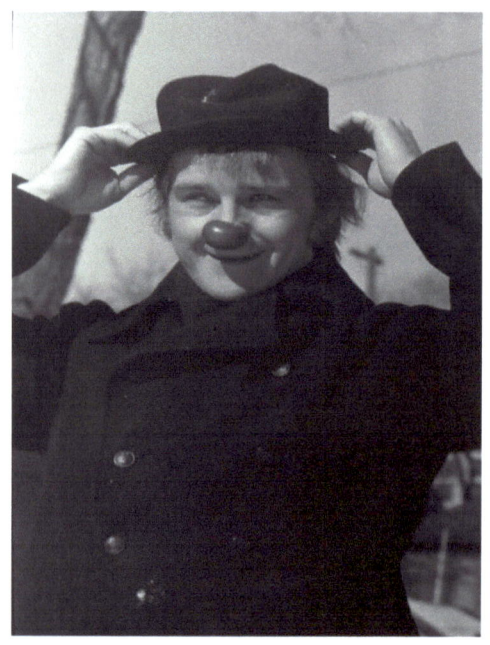

Richard Pochinko as Auguste

Richard Pochinko

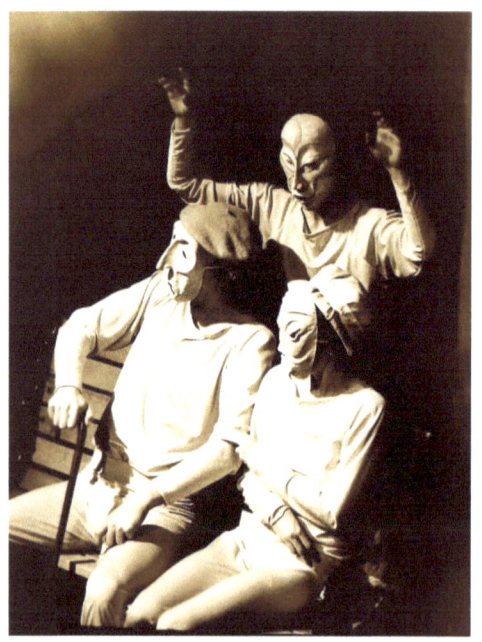

Performance Art by Anne Skinner

Drawing by Douglas Wallace of Jessica

Early photo clowning

**Douglas Wallace
Photographer**

Ian Wallace in Vancouver

Early photos from Ian & Douglas Wallace's library

Judy Marshak & Tom Cox

Michael F. playing instrument

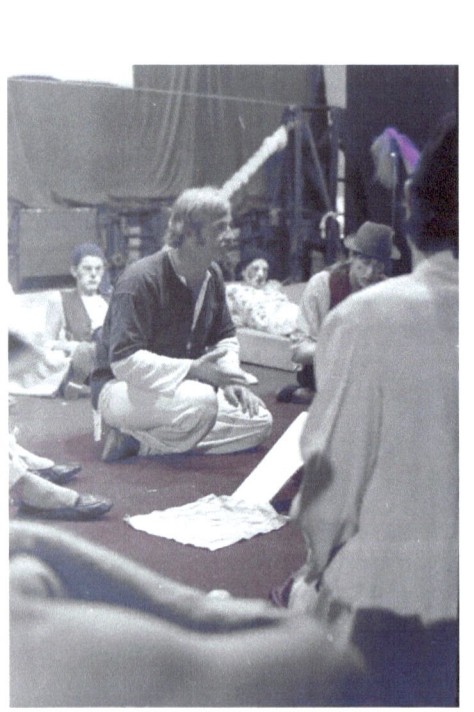

Richard with group

Michael Rudder playing flute

Photos from Ian & Douglas Wallace's library

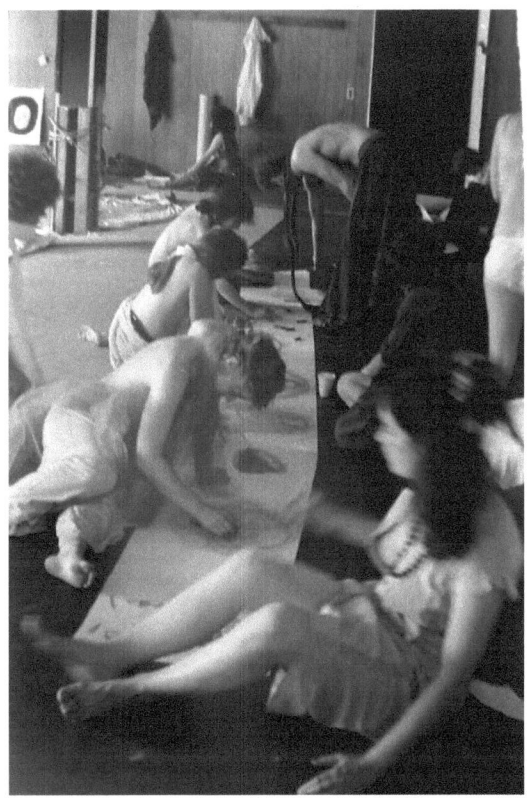

Workshop at National Arts Centre

Ian in Neutral Mask

Group from Clown Cirque in Ottawa

Morning coffee in Toronto

Jill Ornstein

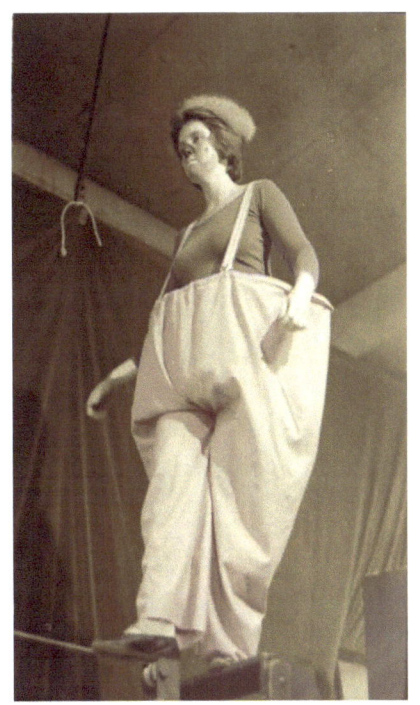

**Judy Marshak
learning tightrope**

Group walk - National Art Centre

Some of the newer Baby Clowns.

 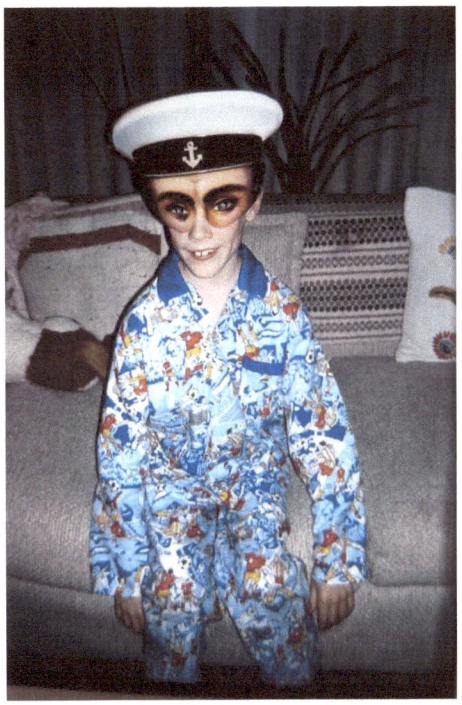

Ian Wallace in Vancouver doing mask workhsop

Nephew - Roy Wallace

Richard working with Pat, Dana & Ronda

Extra History from Paris ..middle "Nion"

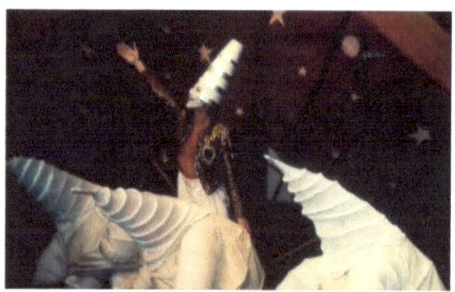

New "Baybees" are born with Morgan Nadeau 2017

Cheryl Cashman   **Jan Henderson**

**Ian Wallace, Cheryl Cashman, Richard Pochinko
Dominic Fecteau and random good friends**

Clam Chowder - Jan, Bob, Marsha Coffey, and Ian Wallace Jan millar

Richard Pochinko - Ian Wallace

**Ian Wallace at Della Burford's home . Vancouver Island
the start of the "book" idea in collaboration 2015**

**Ian in Sicily with his brother Douglas Wallace
(before renovation of house)**

Snake Man -- Ian Wallace

Jan Henderson - Fender - Toronto

Ian Wallace, Douglas Wallace, Bernadette and Landy Lane Marta Roveski and one other friend.

Yves

John Turner & Mike Kennard

Jan Kudelka in mask

Ian Wallace

A founding member of Toronto's Theatre Resource Centre (1975), Ian worked in partnership with Richard Pochinko to evolve the T.R.C. Mask/Clown Technique – a uniquely Canadian approach to Mask largely drawn from Amerindian sources – and to establish a safe, creative environment for theatre artists. Best known for his work as "Nion" on stage and on film for which he received both "Dora" and "Genie" nominations, Ian is a multi-disciplinary artist, bringing together elements of Mask, Clown, Ritual Ceremony, Performance, Video and Graphic Arts. He has played such varied characters as Picasso, Hitler, Jean Genet, Ezra Pound, Pythagoras, Alfred Jarry's "Supermale", "Nion", the Demon, and many "Fools".

EXPERIENCE
Since 1975 Ian has guided extensive mask/clown workshops for the T.R.C.,and in schools and theatres across the country, including: Mummers Theatre, Newfoundland; Niagara-on-the Lake Mime School;Maggie Basset Studio; Factory Theatre; York University; University of Toronto; Parks Canada; Da-Boj-A-Ma-Jig Theatre, Manitoulin Island; Native Earth Theatre;Caravan Farm Theatre; Vancouver Film School; Workshops in the Performing Arts, Van.; "Street Kids" at Station Street Theatre, Van.; Musqueam teens; ongoing (5yr.) "mask therapy" for Friends for Life and People with Aids, Van.; Keremeos "Youth on Purpose" outward bound camp for troubled teens; Xenia, Bowen Island, attitudinal healing & Mask for young teens from the Squamish Nation.

QUALIFICATIONS
Neutral, Character Mask & Clowning with Richard Pochinko for 12 years Journeyman actor, Stratford Festival with Robin Phillips, Movement & Expression, Linda Rabin, Montreal; Voice, Anne Skinner, Ottawa and Toronto; Film Technique, Marushka Stankova, N.F.B. Toronto: Stage-Craft, Neptune Theatre, Halifax; Mask-making, Set Design, Graphics, Painting, Vancouver Art School; B. Ed. University of Alberta, Mathematics & Art. Workshop Introduction to ClownThrough Mask – A Catalyst for Creative Awakening

IAN WALLACE

Jan Henderson

Photo by Ryan Parker

Ian loved the work Jan is doing in teaching clowning. Since she is still teaching the Pochinko technique he wanted to include a resume.

Jan Henderson is one of Canada's leading clown and mask teachers and directors. She studied and performed extensively with master teacher, Richard Pochinko, before co-founding with him what is now the Theatre Resource Centre, Toronto. From 1982-91 she was artistic director and performer with internationally acclaimed Small Change Theatre, literally clowning her way around the world, discovering first hand that laughter is the universal language. Jan is now co-artistic director of Small Matters Productions, whose shows have toured to festivals in Western Canada, the Toronto Festival of Clowns, and the New York International Clown Theater Festival. She directed Fool Spectrum Theatre's clown shows, Please Be Seated, and Silenced, which were well received at the Edmonton Fringe Theatre Festival (2015, 2017). Jan teaches at Grant McEwan University, Toy Guns Dance Theatre, and the University of Alberta, where she has received four awards for excellence in teaching. Her work is featured in the documentary Phyllis's Miracle, the NFB film To Be A Clown, and the U of A films, The Art of Clowning and Clown and Mask. Jan is on the Creativity Faculty of the Leadership Development program at the Banff Centre, and is a recipient of Global Television's 2005 Woman of Vision award. She is a Co-artistic Director of clown company, Small Matters Productions, and in 2014 she was nominated for an Outstanding Lifetime Achievement Award for the Mayor's Celebration of the Arts, Edmonton. Jan has currently returned to the stage after a twenty-five year hiatus in the clownesque comedy, Over Her Dead Body, with Small Matters/Fringe Theatre Adventures.

Jan Henderson .. keeping the Pochinko tradition alive! Thanks!

MEETING RICHARD POCHINKO by Jan Henderson

I first met Richard in Halifax in 1966 when I was 19 and working for the Neptune theatre as an acting apprentice. He was a handsome, friendly, always smiling guy who described himself as a "bohunk kid from Winnipeg ". He was my stage manager on the one show I was performing in at the Neptune and we became friends. I cast him in a production of Lanford Wilson's "Homefree" that I was directing at Dalhousie University that fall. He was wonderful in a part that called for innocence and emotion and endless physical energy.

Years later, I was outside a Toronto theatre on a summer day, working on a street theatre puppet, when Richard serendipitously found me. He had been away in Europe studying mask and clown and had come back looking to train actors. He had been looking for me but didn't know where I was living. The first thing he said to me was "Do you want to be a clown?" and without thinking I found myself saying, "I've always wanted to be a clown". I hadn't known it, but it felt true when I said it.

I took his first four workshops in Toronto and Ottawa. It was wonderful exciting work, but I had no self-confidence and a deep-seated belief that things wouldn't ever work out in my favour. I spent a lot of time despairing and crying and watching him laugh benevolently at me through all my breakdowns and breakthroughs. So I was shocked when he cast me in a clown show, and thus started me on a career that allowed me to find my "foolish" path, and my true self into the bargain.

In 1975 Richard, Ian Wallace, Jan Miller, Annie Skinner, Ellen Pierce, Linda Rabin and I founded the Theatre Resource Centre together Richard nudged Ian and I out of the nest, assured us that we could teach clown and mask, and sent us off to give a workshop for the Mummer's Theatre in Newfoundland. If it weren't for Richard I would never have had the courage to teach mask and clown, or to later direct and perform in my own mask and clown companies. The nature of creative process, the value of humour, the necessity for authentic emotion - I now use everything Richard's approach to clown has taught me in all my creative work, and in my life. Because he gave me back my true self, every good thing I have, I owe to Richard - that wonderful, big-hearted, bohunk kid from Winnipeg.

A FAVOURITE MEMORY

Richard had decided not to officially perform his clown, but often took late night "clown walks" wearing his hat and a nose, to get a special perspective on life. We were sharing a house in Ottawa and late one night I looked up from my desk just as his clown popped his head in my door. When I saw him, my clown heart skipped a beat - and in that moment our clowns fell in love! Fender has fallen in love tons of times in her roving travels over the years, and fallen promptly out of love the minute someone else came into view - but Richard's clown was her True Love, and that has never changed. I used to tease Richard that I was the only one of his female students who hadn't fallen in love with him - but in a way I had!

Della Burford's Student Clown Diary (written when studying with Richard Pochinko in 1986) shown is 10 pages

I saw a poster for the Introduction to Clown from Mask to Clown taught by Richard Pochinko at the Theatre Resource Centre in March 1986.. it would be for two classes .. 3 days a week .. for two months. It mentioned masks, color, and play therapy for adults and that Richard Pochinko would use his personal approach to clowning which combined North America, European and Amerindian techniques of clowning in the search for the personal clown. We would make six masks of clay and learn to play with them to discover our own personal clown. I knew I must take it! I'm in and on! Della Burford

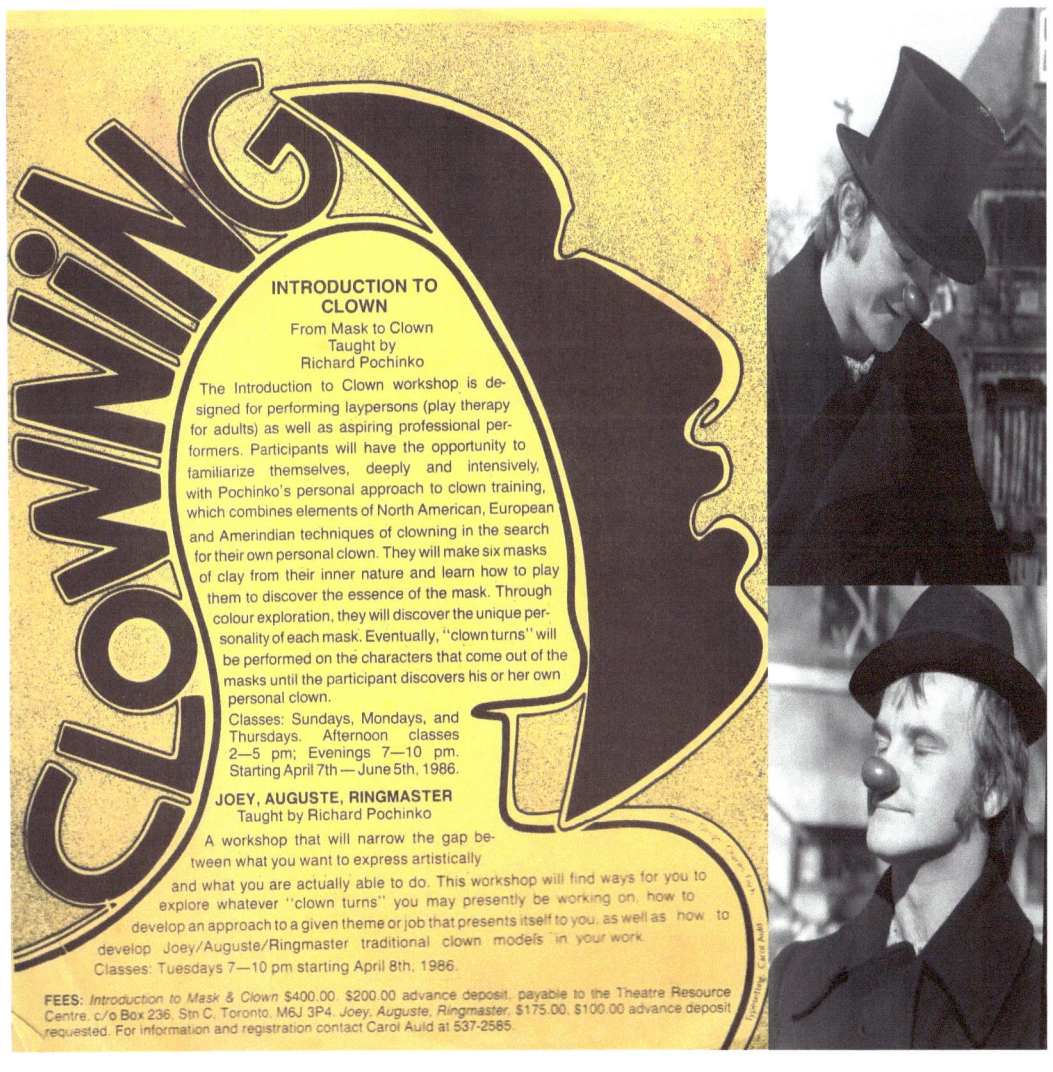

Exploring Color

Wow.. this workshop called Introduction to Clown sounds perfect for me. Love color and like that through color, we can explore the unique personality of the mask. Helping to discover my own personal clown. I am very involved in remembering my dreams and having many lucid ones.
We are working with a shaman who is teaching us medicine ceremony. I have written and painted a book called "Magical Earth Secrets" which is a nature journey thru the medicine wheel to find our connection to nature... our connection to the Mother Earth and in doing so ourselves so this course is perfect. Two of my books had been performed seven years in New York the producer Tedrian Chyzik just passed on to the spirit world so meeting Richard Pochinko and the decision to do this workshop is filling a hole in my grieving. It is perfect!
The first day we felt another person's face and then we had to find the person again with our eyes closed. We made a sound for a person and walked with the sound as we walked we kept walking more and more like the person. The person heard the sound and watched the walk and knew from the sound and walk and joined us as we circled.
The second day we were taken thru color visualization. We did the color yellow. First, I was surprised to find myself seeing this woman in veils of chiffony yellow fabric with sparkles on it. As she danced the pieces seemed to fly in the air. The color was pale yellow with sparks of gold. Around her was light. We walked thru all the different colors of the rainbow. What was so interesting was how different I felt in the different colors. It made a difference in the way I was being, acting, and projecting. Entering a color in the body can certainly influence the way of feeling."
Della April 7, 1986

North Mask

"The second part of the workshop we started to make masks. Richard started in the North Direction. I asked if we were really to think of things from the north and he said, **"Yes, that was one way..but whatever came to mind .. once we started to make the mask a greater force would take over.. the creative force that is greater than us."** He showed us how to take newspaper crumple it up, wrap it into a 10 inch rectangle and tape it with masking tape. This was to be a base in which we would put the clay over. We wet the board and spread the clay over the mound. Richard said, **"You are not to have any ideas ahead of time but just let the clay move and talk to us. You are to say 1 North..fe eh and take it into us and walk around and feel it in your body. Then sit down in front of the clay and with your eyes shut create your mask."**

When I first touched the clay I felt two circles that were eyes - it seemed to be important to me. I wanted them deep. I knew it was looking grotesque and didn't want it to look this way. I decided to put a funny pointed nose and felt very many icicles and a winter wonderland. I made a circle for the mouth and when I turned it around and felt the mask could go either way. The circle for the mouth became another eye .. a third eye. Afterwards, I talked to various girls in the washroom that had a terrible time and horrible thoughts. Confronting one's subconscious .. both sadness and happiness came out of people experiences.
April 18 , 1986

When I wore my first mask, Richard told us **"shut our eyes and feel the mask and put the feeling of the mask into our bodies. Go to the clothes box and choose some clothes that have the same feeling as the mask. .. sometimes they are not perfect but it was a case of pretending as well."** To find the personality of the mask you must feel the experience of the character, say goodbye to someone you love and then go to the child." I found a story developed of an Ice Queen and having a longing unfulfilled. I developed a clown turn. Richard encouraged me to make contact with the audience by saying "more" and "more" when it happened.
May 11, 1986

South Mask

*I created my second mask which was 2 South. Richard said, "**Say 2 South then walk it through your bodies.**" He then drew it on our backs before we started working in the clay. I got a piece of clay and when I put it down on the piece of newspaper I saw a face in the clay. I asked Richard if I should do the face I saw in the clay. Richard said, **"Go with your intuition."** I saw two grooves for the eyes. After walking around and feeling it in my body he wrote 2 South on my back. I felt a lot of green and turquoise. It was a beautiful experience as I felt the clay talking to me. I really enjoyed doing the wavy experience of the hair. When I opened my eyes I was pleasantly surprised to find the face I had originally seen was still there. It was very beautiful and someone commented it looked like a Midnight Summers dream Face. I felt my energy high from it all. May 5th 1986*

After making the mask I dreamt of a small blond boy who helped me thru the process of growth. I had this boy come again in dreams for many years . Once just before the publication of Dodoland and I felt it was a prophetic dream of the man who published Dodoland and soon after this I met him.
The sound I heard was a child's laughter ...I felt a boy girl magical child. It seemed to have wings. When I waved goodbye in experience felt to accept things as they are. When I went back to the child it was born in a flower and a golden child and all knowing. When I was painting realized it was like one done in India in which a flying angel looks into a flower and sees Buddha. (I have included this painting done when writing this set of poems in India in 1974) I felt this feeling again. The purity of the baby and the Buddha nature. In Dodoland (the story just produced in New York from 79- 86) had the theme "to be what you want to be" and the return to the child was very much part of this as was the emphasis to the inner child in Richard's work and finding your true creative self.

West Mask

I created my third mask which was to the West. I just felt blues, purple & space. I think I was anticipating something similar to the last experience but felt a face in the mask that was not human. When I opened my eyes I was surprised to see that it was like a praying mantis or Space Creature. I thought of the caterpillar who turns into the butterfly.. the spirit.. the non face form. The spirit and life of the person from another planet who looks so different from us. -profound thoughts for a non –face. The secret to going home from Dodoland was to say " as a caterpillar changes to a butterfly, I can fly and fly." I didn't see the connection until later but did have a prophetic dream of people spinning on their back and the words above from Dodoland. . May 3rd, 1986 The night before doing the turn of the mask had a dream of a white toad – jellylike who magically turned into a butterfly. then a toad. A reality check on this dream was the day before at Mother Cabrini the kids were all excited because they had found a 5 in. .across moth. It had the ugliest red body but beautiful wings.

When I did the clown turn I remembered Richard saying,
"The six impulses are : 1. Be aware of what you are doing 2. Your body is aware your mind does not register 3. You become aware of change 4. Recognition of what is coming 5. It is coming toward you. 5. Attach or embrace. Breath out of the hands and eyes.
" Upon doing this I saw right away An old sort of grumpy man hunched over .. elfin like who lived in the forest. He was old and his body was saying goodbye to him. He felt this body was no longer able to keep up and wanted the beauty of the other side. He went to say goodbye to the ship and I realized it was him saying goodbye to himself. It felt like he was like a butterfly and there was tremendous freedom on the other side in the spirit world. He was dressed in red-brown like a cocoon I saw the day before at the school and his yellow butterfly was free. He knew what was coming. He embraced his transformation and freedom. May 15th, 1986

East Mask

We did our fourth mask East today. As I was painting it last night and after looking at my paint colors I got really inspired by the mischievous feeling of the red jester that came in the red visualizations and felt it in the mask. I was a little surprised because when I made it was so meditative.
Richard said. **"The feeling is sometimes different than the mask as you do not have to follow any rules."** We could go into one pattern and then go into another sequence. I felt right away the firey jumping energy and heard the sound of laughter. I felt like hopping around and felt very curious and very much the trickster, a magical trickster.
I went to the clothes box and got some red things to tie around my legs, one Hawaiian shirt, a little red hat and some red shoes. Once I started walking in the clothes felt I was a musician and had dark skin. I was very rhythmic and snapping my fingers and going with the flow. I loved life and had the lightness of the jester. They both looked very different but came from the same place of fun and enjoying life.
I remembered before doing the turn Richard saying. " 7. Go find the clothes and hat 8. It's the night before someone leaves.. wave goodby 9. From the original rhythm verbalize the goodby .. return to the house and 10. return to childhood 11. Paint the experience and innocence 12. Find what is fantastic in your character." When I did the clown turn for this mask I brought bananas and they were ripe and when thrown squished. In the turn I became to my surprise like the Incredible Red Banana (my fantastic friend Michael Wesslink) who used to dress up in red with stars and angels wings and who was included in my story Dodoland This was his imaginative clown self who became the trickster in Dodoland and I was his mirror in my East mask clown turn of my baby clown.
May 20th 1986

Below, Below.. Mother Earth

I painted the mask number 5 in the backyard in the sun - below - below. with all the beautiful irises around me, the green grass and pink blossoms. I felt the flow of the mask and felt fluidity. I remembered Richard's words about **"When making the mask : 1. Look for the feeling 2. Create a sound 3. Walk the sound thru our body 4. Touch the mask on your face until you breath the rhythm 5. Drop in the colors 6. Do the special kind of breathing."** When doing the clown turn I saw the tree that came when I made the mask .. yellow, green and cheerful. It seemed to connect to Mother Earth which is really what I meditated before making it in clay. I went to wear the mask and the process was not as definite as it has been for other masks. As soon as I put the mask on I just stood by the window and I felt rooted to the ground and felt like I couldn't move somehow. I felt very comfortable and very peaceful and became meditative. It seemed like the mask was really stuck to my face and part of me. I looked out at the city and felt myself a city tree in a park and all the activity passing by, and the scurrying and the rushing and enjoying not being part of it but at the same time enjoying it. I felt the joy of my branches getting leaves and birds coming to sing on my branches. I felt very well taken care of and if I ever got in need the elemental elves would come and help. I enjoyed listening to the stories of different people who came and sat and discussed their lives with me. I missed this interaction with people in the winter and sometimes it was long. But I also enjoyed the tranquility of the winter. My wisdom of life was immense and my acceptance of life broad and the peace I felt as a tree unexpected acceptance. I started the painting of the tree and finished it outside the next day. I enjoyed having nature around as I painted. My favorite way of painting - outside in the sun. Written in May 1986 by Della

Above Above Mask

I created mask number 6. Richard said to **"visualize the planets and far above and beyond and then come back to our bodies."**
*Richard wrpte 6 A on our backs. I seemed to see mainly the spiral nebula in space. Thinking of Dale and his love of infinity I started to do a spiral. It wasn't so easy to get the spiral even but it was a very peaceful feeling to move the clay in spirals. Then
I finished and was papering it and I did it in rice paper which was much softer and went so well. Moving into the spiral was very comforting somehow. I found out from Eileen that you can do the mask with Vaseline, then tiolet tissue, then alternate with layers of paper towels one play.. and finish with rice paper.. this is what I tried! May 19th 1986*

*In doing the painting for mask six I had a feeling of purples and blue and infinite space. The first flash I got was an eagle with purple, yellow and green wings. He was startling and the power awesome. I felt at some point claws joining with another eagle and spinning together in space like the water eagle does. We have a painting at home of Simon Paul Dene's like this which I love..The image I painting was like it was in my mind's eye. I had very powerful medicine objects around with power that were given to us in ceremony and this helped to getthe energy of the eagle right.
June 1, 1986*

,

Baby Clown is born!

    Each student took turns to go over to Richard who took us through the masks and we would go through each with the snap of a finger and it got faster and and faster until the baby clown was born. Richard said, **"Look at my eyes and do not look away."** *He took me through all the mask - experience and innocence. I seemed to just want to jump and fly and spin and giggle and the group commented it was really like a jester.*
Richard came around and commented on the different people characters that came out of the initiation. He said, **"You are a quizzical Jester and not to stop getting new quizzes and answering them".**
On commenting on our strong points he said **"No one can bebop like you can and not to do it in my world alone but to let other bebop with me. Let them join along".*
    I wore a rainbow hat I had made with bells. A yellow blouse for the butterfly. A red Hawaiian shirt .. white pants and checked socks for mask four. A piece of ocean fabric I had painted for mask two. A piece of the ice kingdom hanging from my vest and one of my fabric eagle feathers for mask six.
  I did a sketch of the painting I saw myself as number seven.

Final Clown - putting on the nose

Went to class and went thru all the clowns to the final putting on of the Clown Nose. Richard said, **"It was the in between the space between the masks that we wanted to explore."** *That this whole ritual was called taking the jump which is interesting because in dreams I have had a woman who came quite a few years ago who said,* **"Now is the time to jump"** *and it is always a powerful statement for me. Richard gave us instructions to start atthe outer edge of the circle in the experience and jump to the center which is innocence. From the innocence of the mask jump into the next mask and in mid-air become the next mask. At the end, you put the nose on and become the seventh which would be parts of all the masks .. whatever parts we chose to keep and whatever parts we chose to give away. "*

When I went into the first mask (North) again felt how proud it was but how lonely. One innocence was so childlike and carefree and easy and enjoyable to be with. When I jumped into the second mask (South) I felt very much the little girl which The innocence of this mask was a crying baby. The third mask (West) was an old man and I felt grumpy at the clothes of the baby on him and wanted them off immediately. I felt such joy to get the brown suit of mask three experience off and to fly like a butterfly .. fluttering here and there and here there and here. Jumping into five was a tree and I felt grounded and observing all of those around and enjoying it and accepting it. The sixth mask was the eagle and very ecstatic and very high and I felt an incredible power and that nothing would bother me or affect me.

Thanks from Della Burford 2017

    I am filled with gratitude for the chance I had to study with Richard Pochinko and to experience the Mask to Clown which culminated in the Baby Clown. In going thru my diaries 30 years later and doing a analysis of 40 years of dream recall (2000 lucid dreams) in my book Dream Wheels couldn't help but see the symbols that surfaced in the Clown workshop that came from deep in my subconscious and some had been in books created and performed and some were yet to come. At the time I took the workshop I was studying with a shaman and I was trained to memorize the ceremonies so I used this to be able to write down the lessons Richard was teaching in my diary. The Shaman we were working with "big thing" was the Medicine Wheel and my story Magical Earth which I worked on at the Wandering Spirit school also moved in a mandala so it fit right in to be going again thru a Medicine Wheel with Richard as a guide. Richard's spontaneity, love of play, and honoring the intuitive helped to reinforce what I believed and helped me also in later years when going through a struggle with fighting cancer.

    In creating Dream Wheels I look at seven years cycles of dreams. In the cycle 74-80 before working with Richard one major theme was transformation .. in the workshop, I had dreams of caterpillars changing to butterflies.. and toads to butterflies and this gave birth to my 4th mask of the west. My third dream cycle of Medicine Ways was 1981-87 and dreamt of many medicine wheels .. we had performance in New York, Toronto and Guatemala. At the later part of this cycle, I studied with Richard and had an auspicious dream of a butterfly landing on his hand. I also was told in 1987 in a dream .. " a transition is made when a mask is put on." Dale and I were both doing workshops on the mask as medicine tools for self-expression and to help the earth thru the Inner City Angels. In my dream Cycle of 1998-94 Wonder was theme and acknowledging the "inner child" was a theme in my work and I saw my south mask of the Magical Child flourish and often reflected on Richard's love of play . In 1995-2001 the Third Eye was foremost and thought of Richard honoring intuition. In 2002 – 2008 the Miracle of being alive was foremost as I struggled and became a cancer survivor. Communication with various inspirational people in the Spirit World who had departed was healing. You can heal yourself is my slogan and certainly the baby clown Spiral mask was part of this. My latest cycle Divine .. I am writing a story with Ice Monster created with North Baby clown mask and it has become the Soul Grabbing Monster and we find out in this story what is needed to keep the world's dreams alive. I was privileged to share the last five years my stories in Bali with Made Sidia's dance company and in Japan with 100% Parade and forsee in the future taking them both on Richard's Baby Clown journey .. thanks to you Richard.. you are loved and will be loved by many. Also a big thanks to Ian Wallace and his devotion for the work. Thank you to so many people who are part of the clown community!

Pat Brennan : Another artist inspired by the Baby Clown workshop

   Pat Brennan felt there was connections between her archangels and the "baby clown work" of Richard. When she did the clown class and small sculptures after she felt an "inner portrait" was being done of each of them and they wanted to join the dance. When she showed the large sculptures - the small "baby clown" sculptures inspired by the "Baby Clown" workshop were shown in behind the large sculptures. She says, "Big connections between my baby clown sculptures, Arcadia, and the Arkangels.
David Type was the model for my first arkangel. Pat has him on tape talking about the baby clown sculptures. David said in the brochure for the show, " From time immemorial , the rescuer, the hierophant, the sage, the buffoon, these primorial clowns have danced our lives and formed our characters. In Pat Brennan's latest sculptures these aspects of the inner terrian each imerge as a minature, each given a face, a form, a feeling. These ar the "cosmos" of the self, each one distinct but - yet entirely interdependant. Whether masked, costumed or anthropo - morphised ; loving, dreaming, hiding, fearing, they are inner faces, they are paradoxically simple but profound. They are the shifting landscapes of our personalities."

   Pat states;"My first Guardian Model was Arcadian, Henry Poesiat, a Dutch Surrealist Painter - (shown on next page). I showed the Baby Clown Sculptures to Richard Pochiko when he came up to the Town Hall for the Poetry/Pottery Workshop. He suggested that I take them on tour along with some of the Paintings from the other workshops.
But at that time I was busy as moved into Arcadia and started making large archangels sculptures of many dancers, artists and friends.
as I said there is a connection between the baby clown and archangels. "
When Pat heard Ian Wallace was in the hospital she wrote " I connect with you and your work deeply. Thank you, Ian, for preserving and developing Richard's Dreams." (writing is continued from a later date on following page.)

Most powerful of Richard's teaching was the Transference of Energy exercise. We were invited to run, walk around the (circus) ring with our partner & watch closely as one partner takes on the energy of the stronger partner. They would start walking the same way!

The baby clown workshop with Richard Pochinko was an empowering experience for me. I was on sick leave from Toronto Board of Education in 1985, recovering from cancer. I was so energized by the visualization experiences that I drew, wrote & painted them two hours after Richard's class – a direct recording of what I saw & felt during the visualization.

I never returned to teaching to make use of my baby clown notes, but several other of Richard's students have used them to pass on the 'magic' energy!

Instead, I made miniature sculptures of my baby clowns. My process was physical – dancing, walking, running with a memory of their energy & gesture around a 6x12 billiard table at my Town Hall Studio.

I showed the sculptures to Richard Pochinko when we did a poetry/pottery workshop at the Town Hall.
He suggested I take them on tour with paintings from the other workshops. I never did. Instead, I fell into making "Arkangel" sculptures with my new friends when I moved to Arcadia, the first artists co-op live-work space in Canada at Harbourfront Toronto. Halleluiah! I had waited 6 years for a unit at Arcadia. The model for the first Arkangel was my neighbour, writer and actor David Type who wrote about my clown sculptures for my first exhibition at Arcadia Art Gallery.

Finally my baby clown sculptures were introduced in Quebec in 1989 along with the Guardians & Arkangels behind a party lifted curtain from the 'Madwoman of Chaillot' play at the Alumnae Theatre. The Gardians and Arkangels were in front. They went on tour as "A Personal Mythology".

I am now writing about my life, art & relationships and The Baby Clown Journal has become the spine of my book. It has been like a chrysalis in my life and work and the book will show connections from my exhibitions, clay multiples, flying canvases, Blueprint Valleysweep to my clown miniatures. The process has allowed me, through drawings & writing, to reach back eighty years to the visualization of myself as a 4 year-old.

Portraits & Miniatures
Friends & Relations, Past & Present
by
Patricia Brennan
Dec. 2nd - 28th, 1988 – Arcadia Arts Gallery

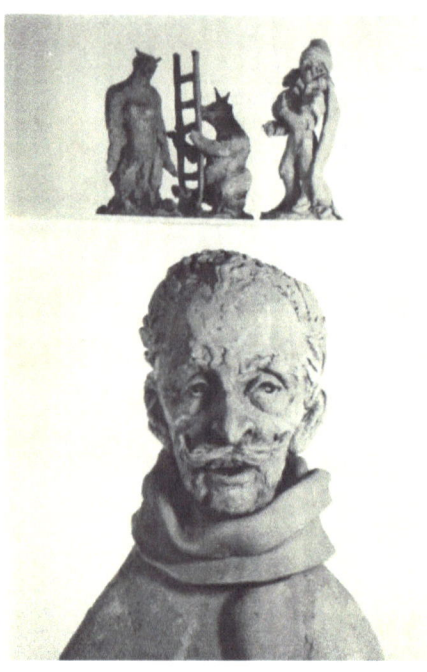

Arcadia Gallery. Henry Poesiat, on the cover, is my first Guardian - a Dutch Surrealist

Della in her Bird Hat - a special Arkangel

Photo montage by Jim Plaxton for the "Footprints" exhibition at Arcadia Gallery.

The "Tribe" of Angels /Archangels

Mask for the 3 West Direction: Leaving home to climb a mountain

Bus boy in family restaurant throwing chopsticks in the air: creating magic dragons

Richard Pochinko 1946 -1989

Richard Pochinko was raised on a farm in Lockport, Manitoba, the youngest of three brothers and two sisters. His father died when he was eight months old. His mother, Annie Napora and his eldest brother Jim and sister Christine maintained the household. It was as if he had two mothers. When he was a child, he would go in the barn and make miniature stages and circuses, and fill them with tiny actors and performers.

He studied clown technique with Jacques Lecoq in Paris, but found the European tradition authoritarian and confining. Back in North America, on the West Coast, he encountered a spirit-guide, Jonsmith, who gave him a perspective on mask from the Native tradition that few people, particularly non-Indians, know. These two traditions came together to form the Pochinko technique. At the core of this approach is the idea that if we can face all the directions of ourselves, North, South, East, West, Up, Down, we can only laugh -at the beauty and wonder that is in us.

As well as being a teacher, for which he was best known, Richard was a very fine director. Part of the reason that this is less known is that he gave so freely, and rarely took complete credit for the productions that he worked on. Many actors and performers would come to him to help develop their work, bringing what was often only the germ of an idea. Richard would pull the work out of them, shape it, help design it, often light and stage manage it and direct it in workshops. Then, in many cases, he would say, "There. I've done what I can. It's yours now." And he would go on to the next new project. (cont'd) (contd) It was Michel Tremblay's era. Richard contributed to the birth of a new Montreal theatre. Together with Debra Silver, Dominique Fecteau, and Nion (Ian Wallace) they transformed an old, decrepit bar near St-Laurent street into a cabaret-theatre. It's name? "Les Foufounes Electriques" There, as Derido Productions they held the Montreal premiere of the play Nion, The Birth of a Clown. To this day, the location still has the reputation for being avant-garde.

Richard was wise, perceptive, and a seer. He was able to differentiate between bilingualism and biculturalism, between nationalism and universality. He adopted the Quebecois culture by offering workshops in French at Linda Mancini's studio among others. If the language got in the way, he resorted to mime. He touched so many among us there. His boundless energy, so contagious, saved many a life.

Resume written by Manseau & Ron Weihs

The next section is various students that were in Richard's workshops comments

Do You Want To Go On A Spaceship Ride? by Jan Grygier

I came to know Richard Pochinko at Theatre School in 1978 – 1980. Richard spoke about things I always intuitively knew but somehow forgot. He taught us to play and to reunite with our creative spirit - our inner child. One day, he relayed a story to the class indicating he had a conversation with a tree. I was perplexed about this notion until one day I realized the trees were talking to me.

Over the years I remember running into him many times and he would be ever so kind, he had that light love energy and was always smiling.

In the summer of 1989 Richard passed away. It was also that summer I participated in some serious soul searching contemplating the meaning of life and wondered what it was all about. I developed a habit of cycling out to the beaches. One sunny afternoon, while sitting by a tree and the water I heard a little bird chirping. Richard came to mind and I thought he was this little bird chirping for me.

Some months passed. One night while asleep, briefly I felt Richard's presence at the foot of my bed as he pulled on my toe to wake me. I thought he was just playing trickster games, he had a cuddly humorous personality. I didn't connect the dots at the preliminary contacts.

One January evening while I was playing music and allowing my closet entertainer dance around the living room floor to the song Do-Re-Mi from the Sound of Music I suddenly felt Richard's loving presence beside me. I stopped and said, "Richard." I felt the room glow and felt waves within my heart until I was completely flooded with his essence. A few days later I played the song again, he came to me and this time he asked me if I wanted to go on a "Space Ship Ride?" – Innocently the little kid inside me said, "Yes!" How can you turn down Richard? That was just the beginning.

The 'Ride' was the beginning of a two-month transpersonal mind expansion trip, that included visions/images, memories, synchronicities and energy flowing throughout my body. It was a therapeutic shift of consciousness; sometimes known as 'spiritual emergence'. I was taught about the world, the universe and myself. Richard was my trickster guide, keeping me calm and playing endless jokes. He took my hand and walked me through various stages of experience.

One day, I was home alone on a sunny winter afternoon when a ray of sunlight shot across the room and caught my attention. The sunlight created a circle on the living room wall. I thought, "How cool!" It turned into an image of a fragmented face of a moon which was eating a hotdog. Then the image became clearer - it was Richard laughing wearing a phantom-of-the-opera mask.

I was perplexed and in much awe! It was like a hologram. His cheeks were robust, he looked great. I said, "Richard?" It was a heartfelt moment and very moving. The words, "You've got to be kidding!" raced through my mind. And I wondered, How do they do this?" After a short while the light vision of Richard began to fade. I said, "Good-bye." The same way as waving good-bye to someone you love in the Pochinko Mask workshop. Richard had come to say good-bye.

If you can imagine words like guide, spirit, trickster, shaman, altered states, holographic universe, quantum leaps and things of a spiritual nature were not in my vocabulary back then. This propelled me to do much reading and growing. I also believe creativity and humour are tools for healing and being human.

Richard helped me to understand my authentic nature, to heal parts of myself, to touch my soul and engage in deep self actualization. I found meaning, a re-focus of perception and beliefs and an engagement with the divine. All in the 'spirit of creativity'.

I seem to do things backward usually concluding that I am the last to know, a fool? We are all connected, things fit together, just like a puzzles, sometimes years later, backwards and upside-down.

I also want to thank Ian Wallace (Nion) for his love, insight and wisdom – his dedication in keeping the 'clown spirit' alive.

*Much awe,
Jan Grygier*

HOWARD JEROME

Richard saved me thousands of dollars in psychotherapy fees. I first met Richard in the early 70s in Ottawa Canada at the TRC the theatre resource centre. I had just moved from New York City to Canada to get away from the Vietnam madness this was 1973. He introduced me to a way of knowing myself inside and out. we first opened ourselves thru the practice of kinetics literally stretching every joint and muscle in our body. This I believe prepared the way for the creation of our organic clown.

We then began our voyage of discovering the clown within After a series of exercises and meditations, we were asked to create a mask, made of clay, with our eyes closed.

When I finally open my eyes, staring back at me was everything I was trying to hide from the world and myself. All of the ugliness shame fear pain was looking right back at me. I was overwhelmed and broke down crying, Richard just came over and covered the mask up with a piece of newspaper; the great shaman rescued me. After I had recovered emotionally he then had the nerve to say to me go deeper find the innocence behind the experience of that ugliness. What I then discovered was a heroism of innocence that was so high that all my shame melted away in the understanding of where that ugliness came from the clown turn that evolved from that, liberated me and anyone who was there to witness it. The Nazi on my back was vanquished, two bricks and a banana settled the issue. Healed thru the power of clown, Pochinko style.

ALICE JEROME

My clown training started in 1972 with a Ken fite workshop. In 1982 I took baby clown with Richard Pochinko. The class and teacher enthralled me as I took clown mask, joey, August, ringmaster; stretch and strengthen your clown, white goddess, kinetics, and clown writing over the next four years. Richard was the best teacher I had ever met. I loved observing him teaching all kinds of people. His wonder and delight in the possibilities of people made me a better teacher when I began teaching clown in the 90s. I benefit the most in my relationship as Howard and I both studied clown with Richard. In good times and bad we put more, more and seeing with new eyes into application. Thank you Richard still.

Robin Craig

Working with Richard and Ian in 1972 was one of the defining experiences of my life, if not the most memorable. It was my first professional job and I joined a wide-eyed, enthusiastic group of young actors to learn, create and tour a show for young audiences exploring the myth of creation. It was mind-boggling and one of the most satisfying personal journeys of my life. Richard's charisma, and expertise and most importantly, his acceptance and delight in all of us as individuals allowed us to explore a part of our souls that had, until then been uncharted. We learned the power of the mask in all of its intricacies and through clown, discovered the freedom to explore both joy and grief in their purest forms. Richard assisted us in removing the shackles of self consciousness and judgement. I am so pleased that Ian will continue Richard's work. A true legacy and even better - immortalization. Thank you Ian.

Crystal Verge

crystalverge@shaw.ca

Richard Pochinko was one of my regular instructors at George Brown Theatre School in 1979. He taught us clown and directed one of the shows that year, "Can You See Me Yet" by Timothy (Tiff) Findley. Fitting that title given the nature of Richard's classes and how much I struggled in them. I hated clown. Hated it. Dreaded class. I wept through the vast majority of them, but I had gotten to know Richard and Annie Skinner outside of class and I adored Richard and I trusted him when he said stay with it. I felt so exposed, not story wise at all, we never went there, but it might very well have been the first time I stood in front of people, soul visible.

Della Burford

I was trained by Richard Pochinko in 1986. Medicine Wheels and inner child exploration resonated with me and felt related to my stories. Our producer of Dodoland and Magical Earth had passed on and Richard helped the grieving. He reassured me that using my intuition was the way to go. As I look over my life of major inner dream work and themes thru writing and painting explored see so many connections to the Masks created during the birth of the baby clown.

Bev Couse
I trained with Richard
comments = I remember Richard telling us the masks would act like tapes, unravelling things in you for the rest of your life: so true---I was there in '84, in New York, in Central Park, with amazing fireworks going off over the water: we were just a bunch of Canadian clowns awed by it--I remember some kids had come down from Harlem; their fireworks were burning rags they hurled around in circles. Cheryl performed her show there, and a famous Russian clown /director was very impressed with the work. It is true that the seeds Richard unleashed have rippled out not just into the Canadian theatre community---I see the effects in so many situation, so many levels: what a rich honour it was to study with him . Thanks
for putting this website
together. bliss................................

Carmen Orlandis-habsburgo
trained with richard pochinko
I the Richard training is still a cornerstone of my life.
I was very successful as Blip in the Toronto scene. From 1992 on, I trained in other forms of shamanism and spirituality. After a heartattack in 1999, I retired from performance. I am now a pure delight maker and live in the ten thousand directions love and light to my old friends!

Audrey Crabtree
I trained with Sue Morrison
comments = I use this work as an actor, director, clown and human being. I work with adults and children in compromised situations where the clown must live in the moment and be present with my feelings in order to discover and play with the audience. It has been a great release for myself and the audience. This work has offered more free play, and a great depth to my emotional life and the human experience. I am a co-founder and director of the NY Clown Theatre Festival dedicated to creating clown community and showcase the range and potential of the art of clown. Thank you Sue and Richard! Thank you Ian Wallace for connecting this community.

Robbie O'Neill
trained with Richard Pochinko
Richard taught me to appreciate the moment and to dare believe that there can be innocence after experience.

Debra Silver
debra.silver@gmail.com
I trained with Richard Pochinko
In so many ways that it is hard to describe... learning to say goodbye was one of the most profound and freeing... and neutral mask began a life of meditation .. and on medical missions it is a true gift!!

Bembo Davies
I trained with Richard Pochinko
Bembo wrote "Ian: it's the middle of the night, having slept all day due to a potential cold caught in arriving in our dirty snow after three weeks in Australia's cicada shower, I have to decide what to do with the turkey defrosting in me fridge. And now this... I do want to think about the seeds planted. For me, a quintessential clown persona who always baulked at the professional role (due to trauma around name?), it had to be profoundly elemental and non-cognitive. -- I think I learnt empty handedness; the lesson of the place of submerging the self to the forces at play, that the clown could follow any impulse and get the goodiest of goods. In the piece I played in Sydney last week -- coming to Vancouver sometime soonish ?-- a moment that stuck with me during my ' research into the power of the Human Gathering' was one of those typical empty moments: swirling in the always half-panicky transition from one necessary unit to the next, I threw out to one woman (there were few out there but of high calibre) in particular - "This is going very well, nugh?" She nodded. This glue, this human glue that makes the performance uniquely tonight's, is the thing. That I finally got my first proper suit in order to summon up the presence of my ancestors, that I speak erudite volumes as I madly deconstruct the realm of the after-dinner .

Danny Bakan

danny@dannybakan.com

I trained with Jan Henderson, Nion, and Richard Pochinko.
I use my clown training everyday. In live performance, in music, in puppetry, in my teaching, in my academic work and scholarship, in healing and spirituality. Now that I am working on my PHD I am reconnecting to my early training and seeing the threads that weave throughout my life.

James Burke

jetburke@gmail.com
trained with Ian Wallace
This work opened a whole new aspect of my life. It has given me strength in performance and in life.

Bruce Horak

I trained with Mike Kennard, John Turner
The character "Cancer" which developed into a full-length show, was profoundly influenced by this work. Approaching, with humour, the darkness in life and showing the light in the world has been
the mission of the work. It has asked more of me than any other form and it has given more back to me than any other work i have ever done. For it - i am profoundly, and forever grateful.

Alan Merovitz

I trained with Richard Pochinko It's a little bit hard to be specific other than , I carry the 7th Mask with me in my life and I often have the clown creep into my musical performances in a very irreverent aspect. It gets me into big trouble when performing with classically trained musicians and those with a stuffy attitude about the interaction that SHOULD be a more conscious respect for the audience. The "Take", is always ready! The send up is very present and the satiric is there too. It is an inter-active feel that requires the audience to be very here and now and I must be . A heightened awareness in the moment. That's it for now . More will come pouring out as I have time to just let it be.

Martha R Leary

martha.leary@ns.sympatico.ca
I trained with Richard Pochinko
I am a speech language pathologist. I work with people with autism. This work has informed my practice, for example: by helping me to see the possibilities for communication in the routine interactions of people; teaching me to seek alternatives ways of viewing a situation; and celebrating the humour & ingenuity of people who communicate in unconventional ways.

Michael Rudder
trained by Richard Pochinko
Richard and I met when we were both working on the musical Hair in Toronto. Through him I came to know Ian and all of the amazing people that came together to study clown techniques with Richard at his very beginnings as a teacher, first in Toronto on Queen Street, and later in Ottawa in an unused part of the NAC. I spent the next four years studying fairly intensively with Richard and that amazing group. Through the neutral mask, I came to have my first paranormal experiences since childhood,vivid experiences of previous or other lives. Working with the character mask, I came to understand, once again vividly,that form follows function. That the flow of life energy in our physical forms creates our thinking patterns and emotional ranges, and molds our physical bodies, and thus our reaction to every occasion or event, and even our physical health. Recent developments in science, medicine and healing modalities only confirm what we learned in this rich environment in the early seventies. The insights I gleaned from studying the circus skills such as tightrope walking and juggling are timeless, and active within me to this day. Richard passionately sought out and investigated every cutting edge physical or theatrical technique, and immediately brought them back into our workshop. His gigantic curiosity and consistent generosity was a lesson in itself.

Timothy Edwards
I trained with Sue Morris - Clown through Mask, Richard Improvization class GBTSI. I did the program with Sue until the final performance where I was not able to attend due to my sister wedding. so I was christened a "Clown Stil-born". to this day if some one counts 1,2,3,4 I am conditioned to revert to my clown mask East of East. I have tried other esoteric traditions and they all end up the same way, loss of the master and the Dark Night of the Soul a al Saint John of the Cross. I was introduced to clown by taking Richard's Improvization class at George Brown Theatre School and we did work with colours and a walking through time where I met myself in the future. It is not as hokey as you may think because in us we carry the wish or desire for the future and these manifest based on unconsious thought in the present.

David Balser
trained with EtienneDecroux
I was directed by him at The Caravan Farm Theatre.
He allowed me to explore and release myself into the characters was playing.and neutral mask began a life of meditation ..
and on medical missions it is a true gift!!

Maarten van der auwera
trained by Jan Henderson
I was born again. I found my essence,through the three masks I made, and so gave birth to my clown,thanks to Jan. She was my midwife,and I will always be grateful to her for that! From than until now,everytime I am in clown it is like being totally new. The world explodes in colour and form, emotions and thoughts,... It makes me settle down in my heartspace, there is no other way. And through this heartconnection,I come in contact with everyone, everything...For 15 years now, I am in the wonderfull position of visiting children in hospitals and old, often demented people in homes,celebrating, loving and taking care...It is an intense process that I share with them. I give a lot,and get a thousandfold back. This has become the basic of my work. This goes beyond theatre,it has nothing to do with "entertainment"(I leave that, with respect,to hollywood) It has to do with being utterly human.This may all sound a bit "new age",but this is what it is for me!

Sara Tilley
trained by nion (ian a. wallace) and Sue Morrison
How hasn't it influenced me? In the most obvious way, I was so inspired and moved by this work that I subsequently trained with nion to teach it to others. I have used this work in my own clown performance, in straight television and film acting, in design, and in my writing. I consider the Pochinko work to be a central source of creativity from which any and all artistic expressions can be accessed. It has also profoundly affected me as a person. I can say that this work is subtly present in all aspects of my life. i am writing a book based on my great-grandfather's letters, and was having trouble owning the voice and the story...so i made a mask, going backwards from key words/phrases in his writing... i have been writing while in the mask, it is a really intense process for sure and the writing that has come out is very distinct, strange, mysterious...so i am keeping on moving the mask work into all aspects of my artistic life, it is a centre of creativity from which i can move in any direction!

Sandra Laframboise
trained The Spirits - the sacred clowns of the first nation

MY SON, NOAH by *Naomi Tyrrell*

The Tiniest Clown Ever

   Noah was conceived at Richard Pochinko and Gabriel's apartment in Montreal, in 1980. It was a remarkable home birth and he was a gorgeous baby although 3 months of colic wasn't easy, we made it through. My friend Dom Robinson came up from Wisconsin to photograph Richards clown classes. He became one of the best clowns in the class. He had a perfect dead pan expression, round glasses and a very cute face especially with the red nose. One of my favourite clown turns was invented by Dom. He was trying to play a piece on the grand piano and his fingers kept falling over the keys, over and over, sort of like a car engine that wouldn't turn over. Finally he goes back stage and returns with a tiny toy grand piano and jumper cables. He proceeds to hook together both pianos and, sure enough, he managed to boost the big grand with the little toy grand for an absolutely grand clown piece. We were all amazed and delighted. Especially Richard.

   Dom had just finished teaching a mini clown act to his friends daughter who was about the same age as Noah and he told me about it. I was intrigued and Noah was game, so he taught it to us. I played Noah's grandmother and I would hand him a sign and his props and I'd whisper the name of the piece in his ear and he would perform it, for example, The Juggler...... I'd hand him 3 balls and he'd throw them in the air and take a big bow......clown band plays da da and Noah was on to the next piece. Love duet had him blowing kisses to the audience and The Acrobat gave him the opportunity to do a front roll. He was a headliner at the Kennsington Clown Festival 1984.

   We often went to perform at Richard's clown classes. Richard used us as a teaching tool. They loved it when we came as everyone was amazed by Noah especially Richard. He would tell the class that they were watching innocence before experience.

   I remember one incident in particular where Noah went rogue on me while riding a battery powered motorcycle, complete with a miniture leather jacket, greased back hair and sun glasses. I panicked and tried to get him back on script but to no avail. That's when Richard stresses the importance of having a back-up plan, or two or three. This strategy has been one of the best learning tools ever and I've applied it in raising kids, dealing with family issues and teaching anything to anybody. Thanks Richard, thanks Noah.
I'm forever grateful.

Naomi and Noah Tyrell

NOAH AND I DID A FAIR BIT OF WORK TOGETHER. WHEN I FIRST DEVELOPED THE CONFLICT RESOLUTION THROUGH THE ARTS PROGRAM FOR JK – GRADE 3 HE HELPED ME DELIVER IT. I WAS GETTING READY TO TEACH ACTIVE LISTENING WITH SOME NEW CHARACTER MASKS AND I TOLD NOAH THAT I WAS SO NERVOUS I COULD BARELY REATHE. HE WAS ALSO PLAYING CHARACTERS WITH PROBLEMS THAT THE KIDS COULD PRACTISE REFLECTING BACK THE FEELING FOR AND NOAH SAID .... I'M NOT NERVOUS AT ALL. THAT REALLY STUCK WITH ME. HERE I AM THE PRO WITH 25 YEARS EXPERIENCE UNDE MY BELT AND I'M DYING OF NERVES AND MY SON WALTZES INTO THE SITUATION AND SEEMS FEARLESS. I WAS SO IMPRESSED. AND HE WAS AWESOME.............

HE HAS A REAL NATURAL GIFT FOR MASK, MIME AND JUGGLING. ABOUT FIVE YEARS AGO I WAS ASKED TO HELP GRADE 7 AND 8 STUDENTS CREATE ABOUT 8 DIFFERENT THEMED MASKS, SOMETIMES MORE THAN 5 DIFFERENT THEMES IN ONE CLASS ALONE. I KNEW I NEEDED HELP SO I HIRED NOAH. WE CREATED TEMPLATES FOR ALL THE THEMES I.E. GREEK GODS, MEDEIVAL NIGHTS, GOTHIC CARNIVAL MASKS, ETC. IT TOOK HOURS OF RESEARCH AND PREP. WE'D GO IN ONE HOUR EARLY, AS THE SET UP WAS HUGE, I'D DO A SHORT SHOW WHICH NOAH HOSTED, AND WE'D EXPLAIN HOW TO PROCEED. WITH ALL THE THEMES GOING AT ONCE, IT WAS BEDLAM FOR ABOUT THE FIRST HOUR AND A HALF. THE TEACHERS WOULD COME UP TO US CONCERNED AND WE WOULD EXPLAIN THAT IT WILL ALL SETTLE DOWN AND MAKE SENSE BY RECESS, AND, SURE ENOUGH IT DID AND THE MASKS TURNED OUT SO WELL EVERYONE WAS BLOWN AWAY.

Remembering Richard **by Jan Kudelka.**

Within HAIR which I eventually joined Richard was not a power. His role was one of stage management. but changing. Various levels as the year unfolded. He was promised the perk of "weighing in on cast replacements." That's how I was cast. Three months in. After nine auditions total. Three of us came aboard. Last audition in the darkened ROYAL ALEX in front of a 30ish John Basset short haired n a Burberry beige trench coat pacing the aisles. What did I sing?
For points?
"When you're weary..."
With all the pushed presence and earnestness Richard would later comment on. But he was my champion. I was one of his choices. It suited that show HAIR. But Richard was not my teacher at that time. He was a soft place to land.
There was a HAIR workshop Richard was allowed to run using the cannon fodder that didn't make t into the show but always held out hope. I was part of that.
Students. Competitive students. In a storefront on King St EAST. More travelling n the bus. The collection of foibles and frailties and unconscious strength that young humans bring to the table is complex and treacherous. Dangerous. Do we meet the right teachers? Are we safe in their presence.?
Richard was unfailingly kind in his treatment. He had to say difficult things and they shattered me at the time. But he was a good eye to his students. Worked to make community . Richard believed in the silver cord connecting us all to the the great Creator/Creatrix that dwelt in nature and sustained all consciousness slash spirit beyond the grave. Not in so many words. . But it was rock solid there. The language he taught was of colour, boundaries, edges of energy and the tools to enter and exit energy. This eventually leading to the skills of taking the " line " into the body and let it shape consciousness outwardly
The mask work. I loved. - I loved it all because it gave great shape and context and palpable tool box to traverse myself, my horrors, my anxieties..
Richard was among my greatest lucks.
His most common comment to me was: "you push your presence." There are two You's and two "p"s in that sentence. It has taken years to understand this part of SELF.
Without the training received by Richard in the post-HAIR cycle., my particular body soul and psyche would have been far far too difficult to live in. I'd have run myself off the track.
After HAIR 69-71, the GODsPELL experience.
Leading straight to Richard's doorway into the cosmos.

HOW I BECAME A SACRED CLOWN NOT A BROADWAY ONE **by Jan Kudelka.**

I am at the time drifting. After HAIR? Lived in a commune on McCall Street. Filled in a role for THE ME NO BODY KNOWS for two weeks of shows before they closed. A stint in the church at BATHURST and LENNOX creating the THOG HAMLET, eventually filmed and now deep in the BUDGE Crawly Films vault, singing on fringes of PERTH COUNTY CONSPIRACY, school tours, bad boyfriends, drifting and deeply anxiety ridden,

Then the GODSPELL auditions;

GODSPELL was the next huge audition cattle call. Many ex-HAIR alumni try out. In the St Anne's church on Dufferin and Dundas. By now I live in a tiny cramped haunted apt in Kensington Mkt just vacated by Murray Maclaughlin. No more long bus rides from my parents.

Audition days ; a familiar grueling grilling. No Richard here. I stay but dis-associate..

They brought us down from 800 persons to 20 in two days. The end of the second day 20 left standing. A final four to be cut. That will leave 12 cast and 4 understudies.

Through a swinging door from the kitchen at the back of the church hall a rumpled fat man with cigar ashes and crumbs on his shirt rolls through to the front and says okay "Listen up! The deal is you're all gonna sign a year long contract with no escaape clause. Who doesn't wanna do it.

Two hands go up. - Mine and Victor Garber's.

Mr Producer barks..."Then leave!" - And we do. VICTOR and I

They call him back to play Jesus. They don't need me.

All this co-incided the same week with a call from Richard saying Canada Council would likely approve a grant application for me to join his experiment in developing a clown.

A sacred clown. A new clown. A vision of clown. A blending of North American Native sacred clown with the European. An exalted hybrid of the form taking the best of each.

After the auditions, I return to my tiny apartment I'm soon to leave. I receive a call from my father who expresses great disppointment in my walking out of the audition for such a foolish reason..

As my mind plays over the circumstance of my day. The prospect of being a social outcast never fitting in a feeling outside in a long running show again for a wage - the way I was in HAIR. Versus what?

Anxiety and outsider-ness making my solar plexus pound day after day. Feeling ready to snap? The thought of sharing Richards dream. Not the redhaired frightening Barnum and Bailey American costuming predesigned and pre packaged predestined to be a left out loser like a high school fool. Even if it was the Royal Alex.- say what you will. I was a social coward. But I loved magic and shamanism even then. More then fame that was for sure.

And it helped it really pissed my father off.

I was hooked. Both feet in, Richard !

For three amazing years

Melissa Aston of Cosmo Circus with Ian Wallace

Melissa and Ian at the Winter Olympics.

Melissa had Ian help her with her "Stealth" boat for her Clown show "Ducks Off" at the Fringe Festival on Granville Island. He helped paint her clown boat.

Dream after Ian passing to spirit world on December 13th 2017 of Ian painting his face as a White Tiger with black stripes. Also shown below is his Jaguar mask and Third Eye painting and my painting Shaman's Eye ... we have a soul connection - happy we could do this project together.. Della Burford

Shaman's Eye by Della Burford

Guardian Jaguar Mask and Third Eye painting by Ian Wallace

www.ingramcontent.com/pod-product-compliance
Lightning Source LLC
Chambersburg PA
CBHW042034150426
43201CB00002B/24